DOLLSPEL

A Raggedy Ann Collector's Collection of Inspirational Essays

Cozette Stacy Nowak

ISBN 978-1-63903-777-3 (paperback)
ISBN 978-1-63903-778-0 (digital)

Copyright © 2021 by Cozette Stacy Nowak

All rights reserved. No part of this publication may be reproduced, distributed, or transmitted in any form or by any means, including photocopying, recording, or other electronic or mechanical methods without the prior written permission of the publisher. For permission requests, solicit the publisher via the address below.

Christian Faith Publishing, Inc.
832 Park Avenue
Meadville, PA 16335
www.christianfaithpublishing.com

Printed in the United States of America

The author is grateful to the following for permission to reprint:

From *Bed and Board: Plain Talk about Marriage* by Robert F. Capon. Copyright © 1965 by Robert F. Capon. Reprinted by permission of Wm. B. Eerdmans Publishing Co.

From *Raggedy Ann in the Deep Deep Woods* by Johnny Gruelle. Copyright © 1930 by John B. Gruelle; copyright renewed © 1951 by Myrtle Gruelle. Reprinted with the permission of Simon & Schuster Books for Young Readers, an imprint of Simon & Schuster Children's Publishing Division. All rights reserved.

From *Raggedy Ann and the Happy Meadow* by Johnny Gruelle. Copyright © 1961 by The Bobbs-Merrill Co., Inc. Reprinted with the permission of Simon & Schuster Books for Young Readers, an imprint of Simon & Schuster Children's Publishing Division. All rights reserved.

From *The Paper Dragon: A Raggedy Ann Adventure* by Johnny Gruelle. Copyright © 1926 by The P. F. Volland Company; copyright renewed © 1954 by Simon & Schuster, Inc. Reprinted with the permission of Simon & Schuster Books for Young Readers, an imprint of Simon & Schuster Children's publishing Division. All rights reserved.

From *From Conflict to Resolution* by Susan Heitler, PhD. Copyright © 1990 by Susan Heitler, PhD. Reprinted by permission of W.W. Norton & Company, Inc.

From *The Notebook* by Nicholas Sparks, copyright © 1996, 1998, 1999, 2014. Reprinted by permission of Grand Central Publishing, an imprint of Hachette Book Group, Inc.

From the poem *"The Meaning of True Love" in Showers of Blessings*. © 1967 Helen Steiner Rice Foundation Fund, LLC, a wholly owned subsidiary of Cincinnati Museum Center. Reprinted by permission of Helen Steiner Rice Foundation Fund, LLC.

From *Johnny Gruelle: Creator of Raggedy Ann and Andy* by Patricia Hall. Copyright © 1993 by Patricia Hall. Reprinted by permission of Pelican Publishing, an imprint of Arcadia Publishing.

From *Animal Dreams* by Barbara Kingsolver. Copyright © 1990 by Barbara Kingsolver. Reprinted by permission of HarperCollins Publishers.

From *Cold Mountain* by Charles Frazier. Copyright © 1997 by Charles Frazier. Reprinted by permission of Grove/Atlantic, Inc. (Any third party use of this material, outside this publication, is prohibited.)

From *Grace Notes* by Alexandra Stoddard. Copyright © 1993 by Alexandra Stoddard. Reprinted by permission of HarperCollins Publishers.

From *Marcella: A Raggedy Ann Story* by Johnny Gruelle. Copyright © 1929 by John B. Gruelle; copyright renewed © 1956 by Myrtle Gruelle. Reprinted with the permission of Simon & Schuster Books for Young Readers, an imprint of Simon & Schuster Children's Publishing Division. All rights reserved.

From a published article on extreme weather by historian Thomas V. DiBacco. Copyright © 1996 by Thomas V. DiBacco. Reprinted by permission of Thomas V. DiBacco.

From the essay *"The Nature of Nature"* by David E. Fisher. Copyright © 1995 by David E. Fisher in *The*

Nature of Nature: New Essays from America's Finest Writers on Nature, 1995. Reprinted by permission of David E. Fisher.

From the *Holy Bible, New Century Version, NCV* ®. Copyright © 2005 by Thomas Nelson, Inc. Reprinted by permission. All rights reserved.

Disclaimer: Raggedy Ann and Andy and associated characters were created by Johnny Gruelle. The names and depictions of Raggedy Ann and Andy are trademarks of Simon and Schuster, Inc.

To my sons Lee and Mark
and
my own Johnny

The Lord has told you, human, what is good; he has told you what he wants from you: to do what is right to other people, love being kind to others, and live humbly, obeying your God.

—Micah 6:8 (NCV)

Faith sees the invisible, believes the incredible, and receives the impossible.

—Corrie ten Boom

Contents

Preface	13
Marcella on *Motherhood*	17
Rags on *Clothing*	39
Pirate Chieftain on *Harmony*	51
Thomas on *Romance*	63
Percy the Policeman on *Precedence*	76
Eddie Elephant on *Memory*	93
The Little Brown Bear on *Body Maintenance*	108
Sunny Bunny on *Nature*	124
Endnotes	151

Preface

DOLLSPEL: A Raggedy Ann Collector's Collection of Inspirational Essays is self-help stuff springing from the wisdom of a stuffed doll. Armed with her precepts, Raggedy Ann and I have teamed up herein to adjust some adult attitudes, to change some mature minds, to touch some hardened hearts, and to tickle some funny bones.

Renowned author Robert Fulghum's personal Credo introduces his first best-selling book, *All I Really Need to Know I Learned in Kindergarten.* The tone of his listed tenets is generally light and playful interspersed with thoughts that are serious and enduring. Indeed, the author's premise rings true—we adults too often mess up because we lose sight of fundamental attributes learned in our youth. My own writing invites grown-ups to embrace for comfort's sake, not Raggedy Ann herself, but what she espouses in relationships—caring and compassion.

DOLLSPEL speaks to basic virtues like benevolence, honesty, kindness, generosity, and thriftiness. These ideals were the literary foci in children's stories about Raggedy Ann and, later, Raggedy Andy by their creator, noted artist and writer, Johnny Gruelle (1880–1938). A longtime collector of the vintage Raggedy dolls and beautifully illustrated books by Gruelle, I am also a seasoned instructor of writing and literature. "Write about what you know best," I have always told students. I have taken my own advice; for I know happiness, laughter, and friendship. I know heartache, disappointment, and pain. I know love, beauty, and contentment. I know courage, spirituality, and patience. These are the things, *essences* of human life, that one will find in *DOLLSPEL*.

To write this collection, I have "mined" Gruelle's accounts of Raggedy Ann's many literary adventures for children in search of nuggets within subjects and situations that parallel topics of substantive interest to adults. Glad tidings from a moppet muse only in part, these essays are primarily literary adventures of a different sort. They are writings replete with varied grown-up challenges and experiences. For example, young Marcella's habit of forgetting to bring her Raggedy dolls inside after play becomes the springboard for an enlightening discourse on adult forgetfulness in *Eddie Elephant*. This particular essay's range of discussion is broad, from the nagging but momentary lapses of human memory that plague us all, to the complex and prolonged confusion experienced by victims of Alzheimer's disease.

Among other digressions in this essay on memory are the intrinsic value of exploring one's past and the secret to leaving a legacy. It is, then, this very *range* of creativity present throughout *DOLLSPEL*—that is, the application *of* and progression *from* kiddie lore to adult edification, which makes this a totally unique collection of essays. Furthermore, as in all good adventures for either little or

PREFACE

big people, the paths that Raggedy Ann and I take within these pages are never straight. We meander and wander here and there in joyful sunshine and bittersweet twilight, even in frightful darkness at times.

Like the rag doll herself, this collection is structurally loose and loppy. The eight essays may be read in any order that appeals. Also, just as *Eddie Elephant* is about memory, the other dolls' names serving as essay titles are subtle clues as to the content of each. Finally, a word about the word *dollspel*—it is a brand new one, coined just for this venture. When pronounced correctly, it sounds like *gospel*. You may consider that another content clue.

In 1918, in his own introduction to *Raggedy Ann Stories*, Gruelle's first of many illustrated books about the doll, he relates just how his only daughter, Marcella, came to discover the old rag doll in her grandma's attic. She can hardly contain her excitement, especially a while later, when Grandma presents Raggedy Ann to Marcella for her very own. Whether the author's account is creative legend or credible fact, this scene serves well as a true harbinger of any real-for-sure person's joy at finding a treasure.

May *DOLLSPEL: A Raggedy Ann Collector's Collection of Inspirational Essays* be the treasure you find today, and may it bring you joy.

Cozette Stacy Nowak

Marcella

The love of a mother is the veil of a softer light between the heart and the heavenly Father.

—Samuel Taylor Coleridge

Like every other region of our country, the South, where I live, has many sayings and colloquialisms peppering its speech that seem to be right on pointwise (however short they may fall grammatically). One of these, namely, is "His Momma didn't raise no fool." It is a highly popular tongue-in-cheek commendation that seems suitable when applied to Johnny Gruelle and his choice of a cornerstone premise for the Raggedy Ann stories. At her inception in 1918, Gruelle ingeniously placed the loppy, loose-jointed moppet doll in a "nursery," which was already quite full of doll "children" belonging to "mother," Marcella. Raggedy Ann was a most important addition to the collection; for it was she who, according to the storyteller, always acted as a "mother" to the other dolls when they were alone. Could he have chosen any institution with more universal appeal than motherhood with which to align his characters? I think not.

The author, who dearly loved and understood children, then turned the game of "Let's Pretend" on its proverbial ear. More to the point, he had it tumbling head over heels, sliding down banisters, shinnying up rainspouts, traipsing in woods, running through meadows, flying in the sky, and sailing on the high seas. You see, when household inhabitants—the real-for-sure people in the stories—were either away or asleep, the dolls came to life and enjoyed adventure after adventure both indoors and outdoors. In every sense of the word, Gruelle's "magic" worked. Children and adults immediately loved the high-spirited, red-haired leader of the pack of dolls, the one who often received this pretend admonition from Marcella as she closed the playroom door, "Take good care of all my children, Raggedy Ann."

Marcella's choice of a surrogate nursery matriarch was a wise one, for Gruelle has embodied within Raggedy Ann all the attributes of an admirable mother. She is compassionate and caring, moral and responsible, practical and efficient, wise and humorous. She can always come up with a plan when everyone else is seemingly stuck (sometimes literally). She can miraculously make a smile return when it has been erased by misfortune. She can build a bridge over troubled waters like no one else. She knows how to be firm without bruising a tender heart. She is ready and willing to slay any threatening dragon, paper or otherwise.

She is most satisfied when selflessly meeting the needs of her charges.

> "The mother is everything," wrote Kahlil Gibran. "She is our consolation in sorrow, our hope in misery, and our strength in weakness. She is the source of love, mercy, sympathy, and forgiveness."[1]

It is most interesting to note that all the benevolent qualities associated with mothers are those same things for which we humans turn to God: the nurture, the comfort, the love, etc. In fact, in Catholicism, the function of Mary, the mother of Jesus, is to reflect the mother love of God; and prayer to Mary is the way to appeal to the maternal dimension of God. Moreover, Pope John Paul I, speaking in 1978 on the proper understanding of the mystery of God, proffered this: "We are the objects of undying love on the part of God… God is our father; even more, God is our mother. God does not want to hurt us, but only to do good for us, all of us."[2] In yet another view, author Robert Capon in his book *Bed and Board: Plain Talk about Marriage* calls mothers the "sacrament, the effective symbol of place. Mothers do not make homes. They are our home."[3]

Combining the views of all three writers, we can say the following: it is our God mother who "makes" our eternal home, who wipes away our tears, who comforts us in our crying and pain, and most importantly, who teaches us how to love. Most women blessed with the birthing privilege will agree to this: holding in our arms a baby we have just brought into the world and being filled to the brim with love is about as close as earthlings can come to understanding the way God feels about us.

How is it that motherhood can be conceived and presented so disparately as both child's play and something akin to divinity? Perhaps it is because mothering does indeed run the gamut of responsibility—from bandaging skinned knees and singing silly songs to being totally selfless, sacrificial, and honorable. Real mothering is birthed from a sacred place deep within a woman's soul. It is but an ember that erupts into a flame that over a lifetime will be stoked by love and strengthened by adversity. The mother and child discover together that, as someone has said, "A mother is love you never outgrow."

Raggedy Ann and her friends welcomed lots and lots of babies into their world—including several fluffy, cuddly baby chicks; four cunning, teeny baby chipmunks; three tiny fuzzy kittens; and one real-for-sure baby boy.

What was that last one again? In a children's book in 1918? You've got to be kidding!

Well, I am not, but perhaps Johnny Gruelle was in an artistically masterful sort of way. Marcella's "dear cuddly baby brother" arrives in the chapter of *Raggedy Ann Stories* entitled "Raggedy Ann and the Fairies' Gift." (To those of you who were expecting a stork, I need to interject here that Gruelle did fairies far better and more often than storks.) Complete in just six pages, three of which are fanciful illustrations, the story unfolds with the swiftness of a ripe apple falling from its sheltering tree; yet the narrative still contains all the anticipation and tenderness intrinsic to human birthing. Accompanying the blessed event is music most beautiful, like hundreds of voices singing in unison. Then *it* happens.

> Little Fairy forms radiant as silver came flitting into the nursery, singing in far away voices. They carried a little bundle. A beautiful light came from this bundle…like sunshine and moonshine mixed. It was a soft mellow light, just the sort of light you would expect to accompany Fairy Folk.
>
> As Raggedy watched, her candy heart went pitty-pat against her cotton stuffing, for she saw a tiny pink foot sticking out of the bundle of light…and a strange lovely perfume floated about…
>
> When old Mister Sun peeped over the garden wall and into the nursery, and the other dolls awakened…
>
> Mamma helped Marcella arrange all the dolls in a circle around the bed so that they could all see what was in the bundle.
>
> Mamma gently pulled back the soft covering and the dolls saw a tiny little fist as pink as coral, a soft little face with a cunning tiny pink nose, and a little head as bald as the French dolly's when her hair came off.[4]

The other new arrivals mentioned above, the critters, come onto the scene in Gruelle's stories in fairly traditional ways, with attendant excitement of their own. For instance, the baby chicks are a product of the old tried-and-true method of chick birthing: a mother hen sitting on her eggs, with a little timely help from Raggedy Ann.

> "I will be glad to sit upon the eggs and keep them warm until you get something to eat and drink!" said Raggedy.[5]

I guess you know what happened while the mother hen was on break. Back at the nest, the chicks were doing some "breaking" of their own, much to Raggedy Ann's amazement and delight!

As for the kittens, their birth was uneventful—at least until its discovery by Fido, who then raced to the nursery at breakneck speed to inform all the dolls after having found the kittens in an old basket way back in a dark corner of the barn.

> "I went into the barn to hunt for mice and the first thing I knew Mamma Cat came right at me with her eyes looking green! I tell you I hurried out of there!"[6]

Mamma Cat's blessed event is recorded in *Raggedy Ann Stories* also.

Finally, Gruelle probably knew full well that he could not have things getting birthed traditionally in his stories without a stork in the picture somewhere. So he put one, full page and full color, on page 79 of *Raggedy Ann in the Deep Deep Woods*. He introduced there his account of Doctor Lewellen Stork, who delivers all the newborn woodland creatures to proud parents like Mr. and Mrs. Charlie Chipmunk. Ever partial to fairies, however, the author makes it clear that it is they who "take the little weeny, teeny baby creatures and put them in nice cozy places amongst the lovely flowers, and when kind old Doctor Lewellen Stork (wearing his magic spectacles) comes along and looks for them, he finds them."[7]

As you know, storks are recognizably associated with the birthing process in a whimsical sort of way; and they have been for so long that few people today would even pause to ask why. Flying high and bearing either a pink or blue bundle of joy in its stout bill, the stork's image has appeared for years now on baby shower invitations, birth announcements, and other baby-related consumer products. Seemingly, in the last decade, yard signs shaped like storks have proliferated on lawns faster than weeds to tell a family's good news to passersby. How very cute! Well, for those who put stock in legends, the stork's association with human birthing is more than just cute and whimsical perhaps. It just may be factual. Among the many, many legends of the storks that exist, here is just one for your consideration:

> With the coming of winter, flocks of storks migrated across Egypt, Israel and Lebanon. One year the storks failed

to appear at their usual time, and their absence was attributed to an unfortunate accident. Then, one night, a miracle happened. Flock after flock of storks filled the heavens with a white curtain. This was the very night when Jesus was born in Bethlehem.

Every birth is a "paradox," declared a gifted local journalist in a touching past Mother's Day piece that I liked. It is both a "natural process" and a "shadowy miracle." He interviewed an aging obstetrician credited with delivering over seven thousand children and to whom, still, the beginnings of life in the womb remain an enigma. That sage doctor stated, "The whole conception process…that's the mystery to me. You look at all those cells dividing and redividing, and it means that somebody's going to have a nose and two eyes and hair on his head. The whole thing is just amazing."[8]

Amazing, indeed! Then the writer himself chose to wax uniquely metaphorical using a marine analogy to describe the birthing miracle. I share his creativity here (his extended metaphor italicized):

> *Arriving from nonbeing into being is the longest and most mysterious of all journeys. On an amniotic sea over nine months or so, the traveler passes through the silent stations of life: zygote, blastomere, embryo, fetus—looking more like a person with every*

passing week. In due time, delicate bones and a complex nervous system having knit together; the tiny mariner arrives, trailing its lifeline and some hideous debris.[9]

This ghastly sight is the most beautiful thing in the world to a mother, I must add!

I nominate becoming a mother, especially for the very first time, as one of those "totally unique experiences," as it is often touted. It is an experience unopen to vicarious participation, emotionally speaking. That is, no woman can fully relate to another woman with respect to just what and how she is going to feel when she first looks upon her newborn. There is really no single word for the emotion. It is joy unbounded, pride unabashed, and gratitude unceasing all rolled into one. The new mother herself is tenderness personified due to her being having been consumed and inexplicably transformed by nurturing instincts over the past months of expectancy. Blended with the tenderness is an overwhelming sense of responsibility, obligation, and urgency.

She cannot wait to start *doing* for this child of hers. They may have just met; but the two will not experience many, if any, awkward moments. Forevermore, the mother will recognize the borning cry of her offspring, who already knows by muffled association both her heartbeat and voice. No longer muffled, the voice and heartbeat of this mother, along with her tender embrace, will provide real comfort and solace to the infant from this moment on.

What has been said thus far about mothering poses it as a highly natural phenomenon—an inbred instinct in a woman to provide food, shelter, warmth, and solace to her child. This view has merit, according to the highly acclaimed child-rearing expert, the late Dr. Benjamin Spock, who said, "What good mothers [and fathers] instinctively feel like doing for their babies is the best after all."[10] I believe this. I also believe that a certain part of the mothering process is learned response. It is a flame passed from one generation to the next. Dr. Spock's advice contains an operative word: *good.* If being a really good parent is about selflessness, sacrifice, loyalty, and honor, then those lacking principle are not going to make the grade. Maybe so. Unfortunately, however, scoundrels will still become parents every hour of every day.

Being a good mother begins in the crib, with a smile and half a dozen hugs every day from one's own mother. Children learn by *example* to love, to be kind and giving, to be compassionate and tender. They are like little sponges, thirsty for the water of instruction on how to be a human being. For best results, the person with the pitcher pouring it on needs to be cut from a pretty good mold herself. This is true because the tie that binds is instinctively a strong one. Washington Irving, a noted American writer, described it this way:

> The tie which links mother and child is of such pure and immaculate strength as to be never violated. Holy, simple, and beautiful in its construction, it is the

> emblem of all we can imagine of fidelity and truth; it is the blessed tie whose value we feel in the cradle, and whose loss we lament on the verge of the grave.[11]

You have got to be wondering just where I am going with this dissertation! Well, I am going to two places: the first is fanciful; the second, frightful. The dramatic contrast between the two should prove eerily enlightening once we arrive. Both destinations will give us insight into the role that sacrifice plays in mothering. In truth, the very bond between mother and child is borne out of her having selflessly entered the valley of the shadow of death to give the gift of life to her infant. One would think that nothing, but nothing, could ever diminish a commitment so weighty. One would think.

There is a brief but beautiful account of maternal self-sacrifice included among the fifteen fanciful little stories in Johnny Gruelle's book for children entitled *Friendly Fairies* (1919), which incidentally he dedicated to his own mother. Mamma Meadow-Lark, sitting upon her nest, invites a friendly elf caught in a downpour to shelter himself under her wing, along with her baby meadowlarks. Gratefully snuggling down, the little elf Thumbkins and the baby birds stay dry and warm as toast and soon fall asleep. Awakening, the elf can no longer hear the heavy raindrops dropping on the mother bird's back; so he climbs from the nest and surveys the scene. Puddles are everywhere; and Mamma Meadow-Lark is soaking wet and shivering, her feathers sticking out in all directions. Big drops of water fall from her head and roll down her beak.

> Thumbkins said, "Are you cold, Mamma Meadow-Lark?"
>
> "Yes, indeed!" Mamma Meadow-Lark replied as she shook her ruffled feathers, sending water flying in all directions.
>
> "But, you see," she continued, "if I did not cover my baby Meadow-Lark chicks they would get very, very cold, for they have little bald heads with not a single feather upon them to protect them! So, while I get wet, it does not matter so much, for I know I have kept my little Meadow-Lark chicks dry and warm and cozy and that, of course, makes me very happy!"[12]

The story ends with Thumbkins returning the favor of kindness that he has received from Mamma Meadow-Lark. He helps her to cope with the heavy rain the next time it comes.

> So Thumbkins ran to the woods where he knew the mushrooms grew, and breaking off the largest one he could find he carried it to where Mamma Meadow-Lark sat sleeping upon her nest, and

planted it so the raindrops rolled off the round roof and did not touch her at all.[13]

Leaving the fanciful meadow on that happy note, I am ready to journey with you now into hurtful reality. There is another story to tell: another story involving, again, a mother, her children, and water. Like the first, this one also contains a mother's sacrifice, albeit of a different sort. Sad to say, help never comes for this young mother, who was terribly distressed by a troubled mind and a gaping hole in her soul.

Most likely, you know this story already. Probably everyone of age alive in America in the fall of 1994 knows this story. Because of what happened, the most common surname in the English language is now among the most infamous. *"It was an awful human tragedy, and it always will be,"* declared the trial defense attorney.

On November 3, 1994, Susan Smith confessed to killing her two children. Nine days earlier, she had driven in darkness to a hometown South Carolina lake and made her car roll down a ramp into the cold water. Strapped into baby seats in the back were her sons Michael (three years old) and Alex (fourteen months old). They slowly and painfully drowned as the car filled up with water and eventually sank out of sight. Susan Smith did this and then lied about it on national television. For nine days, Smith maintained that a man had jumped in her car at a red light, pointed a gun at her, and taken her car and her children. She said, *"I dropped to the lowest when I allowed my children to go down that ramp into the water without me."*

Much of life is about making choices. Mothers, especially, must face decisions every day regarding their children. Susan Smith had a choice regarding Alex and Michael. Beside the dark waters of that lake, she chose death for them. At her trial, prosecutors asked a jury to choose death for Susan Smith; her defenders pled for mercy.

> *For Susan Smith, the love for herself was greater than her love for those boys. Susan Smith chose to drive to the lake. She chose to send Michael and Alex down that ramp. She chose to lie about it.* [trial prosecutor]

When the time came, jurors decided swiftly and unanimously upon life in prison for her.

> *She has been turned away by so many people and has cried out for help so many times, but she never got the kind of help that she deserved.* [a trial juror]

The same pain and anguish that caused Susan Smith to kill her children moved a jury to spare her life.

Seemingly, about the only thing that Susan Smith possessed to qualify her for motherhood was reproductive organs. As a child learning to be a human being, she saw hardly anyone around her being selfless, sacrificial, loyal, and honorable. Rather, she saw those adults closest to her doing hurtful, despicable things: suicide (her father), sexual molestation (her stepfather), denial and betrayal (her mother). Smith's stepfather would say later in a letter to her in prison, *"If I had known at the time what the results of my sins would be, I would have mustered the strength to behave according to my responsibility."*

Being a victim swayed the jury to spare her life, but it does not make Susan Smith any less a killer of her two children. She still *chose* to kill them. At the trial, the prosecution did not prove its theory: that she got rid of Alex and Michael to snare a boyfriend who wanted no children. The case for the defense was ultimately stronger: that her action was that of a very troubled, often depressed young woman.

> *The issue is not whether the crime is bad. The issue is not whether Susan Smith should be punished. This young woman is in a lake of fire. That is her punishment.* [trial defense attorney]

Regardless of intent or motive, or lack thereof, there is no judicial pardoning or earthly excusing what this mother did. Forgiveness is certainly possible, however, from both heaven and earth. In addition, the shame's utter darkness can be illuminated immensely by the light of understanding.

Most of the horror and confusion of this act arises from the realization that the venerable bond between mother and child has been destroyed so willfully. Our first thought is that something almost unimaginably evil has occurred. In truth, the killing of very young children by their mothers is, and always has been through the ages, among the most common forms of homicide. History and anthropology record that infanticide was not only practiced persistently among ancients but was also lawful and without public censure. Our modern, more civilized and regimented society certainly holds mothers who murder accountable and categorizes them as either inherently evil, mentally ill, or degenerately symbolic of familial dysfunction.

Far behind Susan Smith now are the confession, the judgment, and the sentencing for her children's deaths by drowning. Her world is smaller now in every sense of the word and will remain so. Home base is a prison cell, measuring six by fourteen feet. She is assigned menial work to do daily. The system allows her to write letters and have a weekly two-hour visit with a minister, lawyer, or family member. In time, perhaps, there may come some broad understanding about herself and her past. She may seek to know more about her own mother and even other women and men in her lineage. These and others could help Susan to see that she was born into a flawed world that often leads one to make bad choices.

Every human, though, is born into a flawed world. Adam and Eve saw to that. The differentiating factor among us is our freedom to choose between doing right and doing wrong in a moral clinch. Susan's choice to kill her children was *hers* and hers alone. Probing for familial and theological truths may bring to her in time a sort of freedom from remorse. Forgiving herself, though, is secondary to her seeking and receiving the grace of God that surpasses all human understanding.

By her own hand, Susan Smith has become a childless mother. The very phrase connotes a cavernous emptiness, an unnatural separation, and a grievous incompleteness. Is a motherless child equally pathetic? I think so, perhaps even more pathetic. Here is one reason why this is so in the words of poet George Cooper:

> Hundreds of dewdrops to greet the dawn/Hundreds of bees in the purple clover/Hundreds of butterflies on the lawn/ But only one mother the wide world over.[14]

She sounds fairly indispensable, doesn't she? In most cases, however, necessity invents another mother. Matching surrogate mothers and fathers with children is the very *raison d'etre* of the adoption process. If in good working order, it performs always in the best interest of the child. Another surrogacy source that has been around for generations, especially among lower economic groups, is grandparents. The American Association of Retired Persons (AARP) reports that 5.8 million children under age eighteen are now living in homes headed by grandparents; and in about 20 percent of those, the grandparent is the sole caretaker.[15] This trend is now spreading to include many children of wealthier parents who, reportedly in most cases, are substance abusers.

A third substitute mothering source is the overburdened foster care system, which exists to place at-risk children in safer environments. Social workers within a municipality can by law remove a neglected or abused child from home and family only as a last resort. These teens, babies, school-age children, and sibling groups are then cared for temporarily by very ordinary people who open up their hearts and homes to beleaguered children with no other safe place to go. It might be for one night, a few months, or even years. Though far from infallible, foster parenting at its best absorbs the children's pain, helps to heal them, and then lets them go. I would call that the work of very *extraordinary* people!

Speaking of extraordinary, the beautiful passage I share with you now is from a most unusual source. It appeared in the script of an episode of the now defunct daytime drama, *All My Children* (ironically enough) on ABC television. A distressed teenager, Tim Dillon, cries out in anguish for his deceased mother, Natalie. She appears before him as part of the miracle of Christmas.

> "I miss you, Mom. I really miss you. Sometimes I even forget what you look like… I want to be with you so bad!"
>
> "Your mother is always with you. She's the whisper of the leaf as you walk down the street. She's the smell of the bleach in your freshly laundered socks. She's the cool hand on your brow when you're not well.
>
> "Your mother lives inside your laughter, and she is crystallized in every teardrop. She's the place you came from, your first home, and she's the map you follow with every step you take.

> "She's your first love and your first heartbreak, and nothing on earth can separate you—not time, not space, not even death."[16]

What if a child's mother is not dead, not imprisoned, not errant, and not unknown to him but gone from him just the same for most of his waking hours? Where in the world *is* she? She is away from home participating, willingly or otherwise, in the vast transformation of modern American society. Mother has gone to work outside the home, and the times they are a-changin'. Today, with 65 percent of mothers of preschoolers in the paid workforce, the nurturing stay-at-home mom is a rarity.[17] The 1950s was the last decade in which full-time motherhood was "in." The women's movement seeped into domesticity in the sixties and hit full force twenty years later like a tidal wave. Motherhood as we once knew it is now gone.

Quite honestly, the Victorian ideal of motherhood is as outdated today as the high-button shoes worn by those virtuous souls. It may be gone, but it is evidently not forgotten. Two-thirds of Americans in a national poll conducted jointly by the Kaiser Family Foundation, Harvard University, and *The Washington Post* said that, financial needs aside, it is better if women can stay home and care for their families. Regardless of public opinion, the women's movement and simple urgent economic necessity have been sending millions of mothers into the job market for decades.

The ever-present political emphasis on welfare reform will result in an even larger percentage of absentee mothers. The irony is striking! At its inception decades ago, welfare aimed to assist widows to care for their children. The message was that adversity should not separate mother and child. Rife with abuse, today's welfare system definitely needs reforming—no argument here on that issue. However, while our government helps a poor mother to help herself, who or what is taking her place in her children's lives?

A pervasive problem cries out for a solution. Part of the solution here is surely to seek out able surrogates, not baby banks, for the very young child who must endure the pain and distress of a mother's leaving. This, along with adequate preparation and understanding within the context of an otherwise stable, caring familial relationship, will probably make the vital difference in most instances of normal, necessary separation. As in most things, good timing is everything when separating a child from his mother for whatever reason. Becoming a separate self is definitely the plan someday. "But if our mother *leaves* us—when we are too young, too unprepared, too scared, too helpless—the cost of this leaving, the cost of this loss, the cost of this separation may be too high,"[18] writes Judith Viorst in *Necessary Losses*. Handle with care, and proceed with caution.

For about the last four pages now, I have had two little stuffed cotton dolls tugging at me for attention like wide-eyed toddlers at a grocery checkout lined with candy. I really think that they will split their respective seams if I don't let them have their say, which they say is relevant to this discussion on motherhood. Actually, I feel that one of them, especially, has been a *real* doll by behaving quite well and being extremely patient with me, even though I have ignored him during most of this discourse. Raggedy Andy is his name, and tumblin' is his game!

> The two Raggedys laugh at this and Andy says, "Neither of us has a mama unless you wish to call the lady who made us out of nice white cloth and cotton fifty years ago!"
> "I guess I am Raggedy Andy's mother when we are at home," Raggedy Ann laughs. "And he is my daddy then too, for we often sew up the rips in each other's arms and legs."
> "Yes," Andy agrees. "Raggedy Ann sometimes has to sew on a leg because I tumble about so much that every once in a while I tear out all the stitches and a leg falls right off!"[19] (*Raggedy Ann and the Happy Meadow*, 1961)

Oh my! These dolls have a brand of humor all their own, don't they? I find it wonderfully refreshing, though! Incidentally, Andy's brief reference to "the lady who made us" is somewhat misleading. He and Ann actually came into the world from two different sources, both of which Johnny Gruelle documents within the preface to his *Raggedy Andy Stories* (1920). Separating fact from Gruelle fiction, however, can become a bit…er, ah, shall we say, "gruelling." Suffice to say that two very real mothers are credited with bringing these two dolls into the world for no other reason than to make their little offspring happy. There never was an end that better justified a means. Trust me. I know. I am a mother.

The last, best *Word* on Motherhood is from Isaiah 49:15 (NCV):

> The Lord answers, "Can a woman forget the baby she nurses? Can she feel no kindness for the child to which she gave birth? Even if she could forget her children, I will not forget you."

Rags

> And, you know, it is not how we look that is important. What really counts is to be as sunny as possible inside…[1]
>
> —*Raggedy Ann Stories*, 1918

I have a truly raggedy Raggedy! Yes, the entire outfit of the twenty-four-inch Knickerbocker Raggedy Ann is just riddled with holes. It looks as if she and Raggedy Andy may have pretended to be Bonnie and Clyde on that dastardly duo's last fated adventure. Hardly one square inch of the dress, apron, or pantalets has been spared from this mysterious puncturing. The bigger, finger-size holes seem to have nurtured numerous smaller offspring in threadbare clusters, especially on the pantalets and apron.

The rented pocket now exposes far more than a mere triangle of a blue-flowered handkerchief. Moreover, any candy drops Raggedy Ann puts into that pocket will indeed drop through a hole in the bottom. The worst affected, though, are the dress sleeves, the lower portions of which hang in shreds. Let's just say that Ann is now "deruffled"!

Did Raggedy Ann fall prey to some unattended playmate who abused her with scissors or some other sharp object? Was this doll stored at length in an overheated area to its detriment? Perhaps something with four legs and a tail attacked Ann when she was alone and defenseless. I have had to rule out each of these theories, and here is the reason why: the cotton-stuffed fabric doll itself is in nearly perfect condition. She is totally *whole*—with a *w*, that is. Only Raggedy Ann's outfit is damaged, and direly so.

Barring rips, rot, and rodents, what else could possibly have caused the deterioration to this dress? I strongly believe this clothing's culprit to be chlorine. Most likely, some mom of an Ann owner with a bent toward cleanliness decided to do the job right. Yeah, right! She would soak those dirty dolly duds extensively and show those germs and grime who is boss. An overly strong solution of chlorine is *boss*, for sure. Really, the damaged fabrics appear to have been cancerously eroded by some unfriendly chemical agent.

What happened next is collector's history, or fantasy, whichever you prefer. Did the Ann owner, not caring for a truly raggedy Raggedy, discard her to a yard sale or thrift shop? I actually found the doll for sale in a bundle with five smaller Raggedys—a package deal. Perhaps the dealer too was ashamed of her ragamuffin ware, attempting to minimize her flaws amid less rugged, more appealing dolls. In truth, however, the face of my raggedy Raggedy Ann is absolutely ablaze with appeal! How perfectly rich it is with spirit and personality! There is nothing shabby about that smile, no sadness in those eyes. More importantly, her good heart, filled with love, remains intact. It is merely covered over by tattered threads.

This Raggedy Ann reminds me to search beneath humble wrappings for treasures within the human spirit. Fine "clothes," like fancy cars and large homes, have a way of alienating their owners from those less fortunate. Schoolchildren, especially, fall prey to this hurtful fact. Our chalking up to immaturity and inexperience any youngster's shunning and derision of "uncool" classmates is probably an appropriate reaction. However, what of us adults and our shunning and derision of neighbors, coworkers, and acquaintances whose mere apparel we disdain? It is sad when "dressing up" results in our looking down upon others. Maturity should appear in far finer raiment.

The significance placed upon clothing today far exceeds the lowly intent of Adam and Eve's fig leaves! Seeking to do far more with clothing than to merely hide our nakedness, we also align ourselves with a reptile and become upright chameleons. We change colors—along with fabrics, silhouettes, lengths, and textures—to make our outer layers blend in with the environment. Business and professional people, especially the successful ones, are keenly aware of how they dress themselves, knowing that what they wear sends a message. Also, we dress to be comfortable, to have a sense of belonging, and to get what we want.

Without doubt, our clothing is a form of nonverbal communication. What we wear is, for good or ill, how we are perceived by others, at least upon first analysis. What we have on is the first indication, right or wrong, of who we are. Evidence of this basic truth appears even in one of the Raggedy adventures, namely *Raggedy Ann's Wishing Pebble* (1925):

> "I always thought that Gerty Gartersnake wore her dresses much too tight!" Mister Muskrat said with a sly wink at Raggedy Andy.[2]

Looking good equates with feeling good for some people. Self-esteem enhancement is just one coordinated outfit away. To many, happiness is shopping for clothing till they drop onto a pile of packages. Neither of these attitudes about attire is reprehensible until one who caters to clothes allows his fashion sense to override his sense of goodness toward others. Raggedy Ann, on the other hand, would have us give the person underneath the clothing a chance. She would admonish us to practice uncondescending kindness, something that never goes out of style.

Johnny Gruelle explores this very premise in one of his first stories about our cotton-clad heroine. In *Raggedy Ann Stories*, a beautiful new doll named Annabel-Lee arrives in Marcella's nursery. "Annabel was dressed in soft, lace-covered silk and upon her head she wore a beautiful hat with long silk ribbons tied in a neat bow-knot beneath her dimpled chin,"[3] writes Gruelle. From the onset, this finely dressed doll's favorite pastime was ridiculing Raggedy Ann's ungainly appearance: "'She looks like a scarecrow!' said Annabel-Lee, as she primped her dress."[4]

Because Marcella yet had no nightie or bed for it, she left the new doll to fall asleep that first night sitting in a chair in all her finery. However, kind Raggedy Ann, as Gruelle relates, "slipped quietly from her [own] bed and… tiptoed to the…beautiful new [doll]." Assisted by Uncle Clem, she "lifted [Annabel-Lee] gently so as not to awaken [her] and carried [her] to Raggedy Ann's bed. She tucked [Annabel-Lee] in snugly and lay down [herself] upon the hard floor." Day's dawning brought with it the realization to Annabel-Lee that "Raggedy Ann had generously given [up] her bed."[5] What a beautiful example this is of unselfishly turning the other cheek!

My special rag doll prompts me also to recall Raggedy Ann's lowly roots. Johnny Gruelle had two sources of inspiration for naming his artistic offspring in 1915. These were "The Raggedy Man" and "Little Orphant Annie," both poetic creations of James Whitcomb Riley, a close friend of the Gruelle family in years past in Indiana. To further honor Riley and to further his own career, in 1921, Gruelle labored excitedly over separate illustrated books based on these two characters.

He completed only the *Orphant Annie Story Book*, which is comprised of ten original fairy stories told by Annie to the eager ears of Carl and Bessie, youngsters in the fictional family with whom Annie had come to live and work. The publication abounds with beautiful word and picture illustrations from the mind, heart, and hand of Johnny Gruelle. He describes Annie as "a thin, poorly clad girl," whose wretched appearance brought tears to the eyes of the children's mother when she first saw her.

Gruelle continues with a vivid head-to-toe description of Annie's outfit:

> Her hat…was a funny, old summer hat with a bunch of faded flowers twisted about the crown and held in place with heavy black linen thread… Mother… untied the green veil that held Orphant Annie's hat on her head and unpinned the tattered shawl from around her shoulders…she must be very cold. Her little hands were covered with mittens, made from old stockings, that were so short they left the wrists showing bare and blue. Orphant Annie's shoes, as the children afterward learned, had belonged to her aunt and were so large they could easily have held feet twice the size of Orphant Annie's, while the toes turned up just as do the shoes worn by Turkish women.[6]

Finally, Gruelle, the artist, renders a full-page color portrait of this little girl that positively wrenches the beholder's heart. Orphant Annie, with her large frightened eyes, becomes every child, the embodiment of innocence. Luckily, her kindly surrogate family of four willingly gave this little person in the ragged clothing a chance. In time, Orphant Annie reportedly "proved a willing, cheerful, hearty worker"; and the children "grew to love her." Raggedy Ann can be justifiably proud of this namesake!

Could it be that a humble beginning, like a hardening period for plants, makes us stronger in character? Are we perhaps less quick to bend with the wind of public opinion and more inclined to be our own person, a person worth knowing? Such was surely the case for these two little fictional ragamuffins! Here is an often-repeated characterization of one of them: "Raggedy Ann was the first to remember that it is not good manners to laugh at a person because of the way he looks"[7] (*Raggedy Ann and the Golden Ring*, 1961). We do not have to wonder where she learned that!

Although Johnny Gruelle wrote no entire book devoted to Riley's "The Raggedy Man," Ann's other inspiration, he otherwise immortalized this colorful character. The third chapter of *Orphant Annie Story Book* is a fine example, complete with wistful pictures, of Gruelle's "ragman," a kind and gentle soul who never "even spoke crossly to" his horse.

> "But there were people in the town who did not like the rag-man," wrote Gruelle. "It may have been because he was just a rag-man, or it may have been because he was poor and did not live in a fine house and wear fine clothes as they did."[8]

Sometimes it just takes a little harmless "whangwhizzling," as Gruelle described it, to turn folks around, doesn't it? This sterling individual does eventually get to bask in the sunlight of kindness from everyone. Raggedy Ann would surely add quickly, "And he's worth it!"

Indeed, to evaluate someone solely on the basis of outward appearance is to negate his innate worth as a person. What a shame! Pity the poor perpetrator, however, not the shunned one. Who knows how many lives are daily less enriched because of self-imposed caste systems?

I am reminded of an acquaintance who realized a dream of starting her own business. With its quick success, the demands upon her time became so overwhelming that her beloved yard and garden at home became nightmares to behold! Curiously, at her door one weekend appeared someone who could have doubled for Gruelle's rag-man, by my friend's description. The caller claimed to be a "yard man" and said that he had noticed in passing by that her yard needed some attention. She decided that he was at least half-right, without question!

Wary of his disheveled appearance but desperate for help, she hired him, knowing full well that he would usually have to be working around her home when she was not there. How else could he ever have restored that property to better-than-before-bum condition and kept it that way? He designed and effected a grape arbor, a rock wall, and a goldfish pond for her grandson to enjoy; he also created an herb garden *and* produced winding paths leading to brand new beauty spots in her yard. In a word, the bum, to some observers, was a blessing in disguise to my friend. And that's just what she calls him, Blessing, for he has never given her another name.

Johnny Gruelle was fond of creating story lines for children proving that appearances can be deceiving. Such a dichotomy afforded his young audience the opportunity to laugh and learn simultaneously. Near the end of *Raggedy Ann and Andy and the Camel with the Wrinkled Knees* (1924), the Pirates turn out to be pretty girls and the Witch, a Fairy Princess. All along, each of the ornery characters has honorable intentions in the adventure; they merely look the part of villains. Kindness from others leads to their eventual restoration and this inspiring verbal exchange:

> "But one can really never tell by appearances," Raggedy Andy said.
> "That is indeed true," the Fairy Princess laughed. "But so many persons always judge people by the way in which they are dressed. Why, the ugliest shell may be hiding the most beautiful pearl and the roughest cover may be on the loveliest, sweetest story book. It isn't what is on the outside that counts; it is what we may have within us."[9]

A thought-provoking television commercial produced by the Cotton Council of America once aired in my region. It spoke musically of "the fabric of our lives" and showed rapid scenes of ordinary people enveloped in everyday events, both woeful and wonderful. I was reminded by this advertisement that human life is indeed a sort of tapestry, woven of the brighter threads of gladness intermingled with darker strands of sorrow. The following beautiful old poem of disputed authorship conveys the same idea:

> My life is but a weaving
> Between my Lord and me,
> I cannot choose the colors
> He worketh steadily.
> Oftimes he weaveth sorrow,
> And I in foolish pride
> Forget He sees the upper
> And I, the underside.
> Not till the loom is silent
> And the shuttles cease to fly
> Shall God unroll the canvas
> And explain the reason why.
> The dark threads are as needful
> In the Weaver's skillful hand
> As the threads of gold and silver
> In the pattern He has planned.[10]

The wealthiest among us cannot afford garments made entirely of the more illuminating threads. That is, just the brighter, more joyous life experiences cannot be all that we have. The rich and powerful too must endure hurt and loss and pain in their lives. Every person's wardrobe includes the sackcloth of sorrow. Jacqueline Kennedy Onassis, at only sixty-four, had to forfeit the quality and quantity of her years to cancer. Hence, the often-beleaguered Kennedy family gathered once more to say goodbye to a loved one taken too soon.

Life's unkind experiences, no respecters of persons, often leave us tattered and torn. As we mend these emotional rents, we realize that responding to adversity is a task for one and all, old and young, rich and poor. However, I believe that the human spirit is up to the challenge. You and I are in possession of a marvelous resiliency that is capable of restoring the most threadbare of souls. The secret lies in our *wanting* to be happy—or "sunny," as our little raggedy heroine is fond of saying. Explicitly, she tells us, "Never give up hope… Always feel and know that the sun is shining above the darkest of rain clouds and that with the passing of the rain, we shall see the gleaming of the rainbow"[11] (*Raggedy Ann's Lucky Pennies*, 1932).

Raindrops will surely keep falling on our heads. Trials *will* come. However, sunshine after the rain is so natural and so necessary. Resolve to move forward in the face of difficulty; and consciously decide to be happy, to enjoy what you have. Do not persevere wearily, but persevere with a smile. Accepting loss and disappointment without bitterness comes with simply understanding that heartache is a part of the human condition. The question is never whether or not we will meet adversity but rather how we will deal with it *when* it comes.

I hope that you will wear them well, the trappings of trial and tragedy that you are handed. Like my little raggedy Raggedy Ann, whenever you are punctured by adversity, let there be no shabbiness in your smile, no sadness in your eyes. Let the world know that your own good heart, filled with love, remains intact. It is merely covered over by tattered threads.

The last, best *Word* on Clothing is from 1 Samuel 16:7 (NCV):

> But the Lord said to Samuel, "Don't look at how handsome Eliab is or how tall he is, because I have not chosen him. God does not see the same way people see. People look at the outside of a person, but the Lord looks at the heart."

Pirate Chieftain

> You mustn't fight! It isn't nice to quarrel and fight like cats and dogs![1]
>
> —*The Paper Dragon: A Raggedy Ann Adventure*, 1926

We have it upon good authority from her creator, Johnny Gruelle, that Raggedy Ann, "no matter what happened, never lost her temper"[2] (*Raggedy Andy Stories*, 1920). I found this statement a bit incredulous since she and Raggedy Andy must contend with so many ornery characters in their adventures! Nobody's perfect, you know. So I just read on, keeping my eyes and ears open for anything smacking of a riled Raggedy. And sure enough…

"Now!" cried Raggedy Ann, as she stamped her rag foot. "Why did you take the Dragon away from us, Mr. Doodle?

> Just tell me that!"³ (*The Paper Dragon: A Raggedy Ann Adventure*, 1926)

Hmmm… Voice-raising and foot-stamping surely sound like temper-losing to me. Uh, oh. Looks as if we need to add fist-shaking to that list of gestures.

> "Now, see here," Raggedy Ann said, shaking her hand under the Wizard's long nose.⁴ (*Raggedy Ann and the Hobby Horse*, 1961)

Better a fist under the nose than a broom over the head. Read on.

> Just then Raggedy Ann brought the broom down on the little old man's head with a THUMP.⁵ (*Raggedy Ann and Andy and the Nice Fat Policeman*, 1942)

Oh, well. Raggedy Ann is a redhead (and we all know just how fiery they can get at times). Before sunset in the Deep Deep Woods, however, all is always well again.

Similarly, Raggedy Ann would have us quickly bandage the emotional wounds that we inflict upon others and vow to "try never again to do anything which might cause those who love us any unhappiness of any kind"⁶ (*Raggedy Ann Stories*, 1918). Such is an admirable goal, but somehow, peaceful coexistence has always been a tall order for us grudge-bearing humans.

PIRATE CHIEFTAIN

Ever so contemporary is the term *fallout*, a nuclear power by-product that generally descends highly charged, leaving potential destruction in its wake. Far from modern but just as malign is *falling-out*, a condition powered by humans. These two terms' similarities extend beyond mere nomenclature to incorporate both definition and implication. Think about it. A quarrel between friends or a rift among family members, a falling-out, also "descends highly charged, leaving potential destruction in its wake."

Angry words and bitter accusations, as numberless as radioactive particles, are spewed from the mouths of the emotionally injured. Moreover, just like those descending fallout particles, the anger and accusations can never be retrieved once they are let loose. Having settled, they become most unsettling and can only be dealt with. Carl Sandburg once penned a nice little poem on this very big subject. He called it "Primer Lesson."

> Look out how you use proud words.
> When you let proud words go, it is not easy to call them back.
> They wear long boots, hard boots; they walk off proud; they can't hear you calling—
> Look out how you use proud words.[7]
> (from *Smoke and Steel and Slabs of the Sunburnt West*, 1920)

Words are indeed powerful. A moving *Touched by an Angel* episode on CBS Television dealt with a small boy whose "hobby" was words. He mastered with ease the pronunciation, definition, and spelling of the most difficult words; yet he viewed himself as worthless, especially when compared to his star-athlete brother. Coming to the troubled youngster's aid, the angels reminded him that God created the world through words. Every day we humans also create with words. Written and spoken, our words evoke the deepest emotions possible, leading us often to love but sometimes also to hatred and terrible pain.

"Sticks and stones can break my bones, but words can never hurt me," so the saying goes. No child subjected to verbal abuse from parent or peer believes that little ditty, nor does any adult of minority ethnicity or policeman branded with derisive labels that depict them as subhuman. What of this equally familiar saying, "Do unto others as you would have them do unto you"? Sadly, the golden rule becomes tarnished more often by foul human speech than by any other means of transgression.

Really "good" people, folk who would never rob or kill another, systematically use words irresponsibly and cruelly. Consider your own experiences. Excluding any terrible physical violence that you or a loved one has endured, probably the very worst pain in your life has come from someone's cruel use of language. All too often, we criticize others with harsh, offensive words. We turn disputes into quarrels, we belittle and humiliate others, and we inflict wounds that last a lifetime.

This caustic conduct is costly, it would seem. Siblings refuse to speak to one another. Spouses no longer communicate on any level. Former friends betray confidences. Coworkers shun each other. There has been a falling-out, you see. So much resentment, negativity, and vengeance give birth in time to a grudge. *Time* is now the operative word, for some grudges within families have been known to span entire generations. As time passes, grudges rankle and fester, like so many lesions upon the human heart. Sadly, they are proven infectious and highly communicable.

"I think of a grudge as a combination of garbage and sludge," says Susan Heitler, a psychologist from Denver and the author of *From Conflict to Resolution*.[8] "It's a resentment or old negative feelings that we have in response to something unpleasant that happens," she continues. How apt of that idiomatic usage, implying us to be "carrying" or "holding" onto grudges like so much excess baggage! They certainly can weigh us down, taking their toll upon us both psychically and physically. Holding onto a grudge is a constant, simmering anger that can burn one up inside. It is never a healthy state of affairs. The truth is that the longer we hold onto something, the more it becomes a part of us. If it is a putrid something, like a grudge…well, you get the picture.

Another fact of life is that we humans feel the need to hold onto things for security's sake. Understandably, on a roller coaster, most of us hold on so tightly that our hands hurt. On the crazy rides we take in life, like grudge bearing, we do likewise—except holding on hurts our hearts. Why not let go of the bar and feel free? Get the full effect of the ride! "Let go and let God," as the saying goes. Getting past the grudge is vital. It is a feat that can be accomplished, according to Dr. Heitler, in one of two ways: either make up with the person, or eject the person from your life. Either way will result in a healthier, happier you.

Major concerns, no matter how petty, precipitate all strife between humans. The catalyst for every disagreement is paramount to someone involved. Rank aside, the reason for dissension sometimes gets lost in the shuffle (or scuffle), I have noticed. That is, among some who have been in a falling-out, after a while, contention for contention's sake takes precedence over the point of contention itself. "This is *my* argument, and nobody's gonna take it away from me!" is the apparent battle cry.

In truth, someone to "take away" the argument, an arbitrator, is sometimes just what is needed. Fair, effective mediation requires a *neutral* observer—someone to stand outside the hazy window of discord and peer within. Eventually, good judgment can begin to wipe away the distortion. Those inside the argument may then view more clearly the total picture.

Raggedy Ann spends much of her time as an adventuress just settling disputes among bickering adversaries of her acquaintance. She is an arbitrator *par excellence*. Who would know better than her creator? Gruelle wrote of her, "Raggedy Ann usually thought of the best way of doing everything"[9] (*The Paper Dragon: A Raggedy Ann Adventure*, 1926). Surprisingly, she gets little assistance from Raggedy Andy.

Being much too quick to want to "rassle" the bad guys, Andy often becomes a part of the problem! For example, when Old Whoosey, a mean little man, steals the left-handed safety pin in the story by the same name (1935); Andy's first thought is to floor the scoundrel and retrieve it. To make matters worse and to Ann's chagrin, Andy never gives up in a match until he has wrestled the best! This is why a resigned Raggedy Ann says to the good little witch who owns the safety-pin charm, "We may as well go over and sit in comfortable chairs until it is over."[10]

Everyone knows that to win, any good wrestler simply wears down his opponent. Raggedy Andy, stuffed with soft cotton, could neither send nor receive really harmful blows. However, he could send and send *and* send them and receive and receive *and* receive them until the other guy (stuffed with who knows what) becomes exhausted from sheer persistent resistance! Mr. Whoosey, no exception in this particular scuffle, eventually says meekly (and weakly), "I don't wish to wrestle anymore."[11]

The likes of old Whoosey, Mr. Doodle, Toofie, Minkie, Gilly Imp, Bugaboo, and other sundry misfits sprang from Johnny Gruelle's imagination and into actions intended to cause malevolent reactions. Conflict is so essential to a good story, though. This, Gruelle knew. He knew too that his "books good for children" could not ultimately "glorify mischief, excuse malice, or condone cruelty." Hence, redemption for these rascals always arrives before an adventure's end. Raggedy Ann is the special deliverer, the soft, cottony voice of reason. Her peacemaking admonitions make sense; one worth remembering is "we must never hurt others even when they are mean to us"[12] (*Raggedy Ann's Wishing Pebble*, 1925). Didn't we hear that advice before, more than two thousand years ago?

Even more admirable than seeking external arbitration to resolve differences is having one involved in the dispute to step forward and say, "Enough is enough!" He or she has come to understand the alienation for what it is: a sickening separation fed by selfishness and pride, the antidote for which is plain old forgiveness.

Undeniably, the seeds that produce our forgiving and our unforgiving natures are sown during childhood. We learn by example, I believe, to be hateful, spiteful, and argumentative. Conversely, we also imitate models who are kind, generous, and loving. The experts say that some people are born with a proclivity toward negativism, an arguable theory contrasting the "clean slate at birth" theory. Nevertheless, loud voices wanting their own way have a way of reverberating from youth to adulthood.

Children so easily adopt as their own the actions and attitudes that they see and hear. A parent's or guardian's constant arrogance and impetuosity will nullify rather than nurture within a child the skills needed to settle disagreements. Such home-front exposure, coupled with the insistent ego's natural emergence somewhere in toddlerhood, provides a climate in which controversial personalities thrive. Perhaps in homes with little ones, it would be a good idea to post somewhere conspicuous a placard that reads, "Quiet please. Children are listening and learning."

I read of a man in his fifties who embraced racial activism and whose friends readily described him as having an "ax to grind" or a "chip on his shoulder" most of the time. To the interviewer, he admitted, "The thing about anger is that you have to find someplace to *put* it." When asked if he could ever just let the anger go (dissipate), he replied, "Impossible. It's the only me I know. Anger defined me as a child." He said slowly, "This is how I was made. I'd have to unmake myself and start over." At middle age, it is very difficult, I say, but certainly not impossible—with the right Personal Trainer.

The man is spiritually malnourished and exhausted, having eaten, slept, and breathed rage for so long. His salvation would be to come by a gratitude for life itself, to be joyful. Anger does as much damage to the vessel in which it is stored as it does to whatever it is poured out upon. Let's allow Raggedy Andy to put it another way: "Whenever you try to injure another, you always harm yourself"[13] (*The Paper Dragon,* 1926). Anger depletes while joy energizes and renews.

Renewing is starting over. Didn't I tell you it was not impossible? Now, I have proof more tangible! One day in 1989, syndicated columnist Ann Landers received among her hundreds of letters a poignant outpouring from a forty-one-year-old California woman. The latter enumerated just how she and her large family, as well as several personal friends, had become variously estranged over the years by numerous hurt feelings and misunderstandings. Barriers were all around to prevent the flow of love—love that she longed for more and more as she and they aged. The years now seemed to be flying by, and grievances of long ago were robbing everyone of precious togetherness time. Here, in her own words, is the rest of what this reader wrote to Ann Landers:

> Ann, I'm sure millions of people in your reading audience could tell similar stories. Wouldn't it be terrific if a special day could be set aside to reach out and make amends? We could call it "Reconciliation Day." Everyone would vow to write a letter or make a phone call and mend a strained or broken relationship. It could also be the day on which we would all agree to accept the olive branch extended by a former friend. We could go on from here to heal the wounds in our hearts and rejoice in a new beginning.[14]

This was one time that Ann Landers *took* advice from a reader! The very first Reconciliation Day was April 2, 1989, the same day that the famous columnist (now deceased) first published the suggestion and her own beautiful response to it, which read in part as follows:

> Life is too short to hold grudges. To be able to forgive can be enormously healing and life enhancing. It's the best example of casting your bread upon the waters and getting back caviar sandwiches. Do it today.[15]

As you might expect, Ann reported over the ensuing years that she had received hundreds of heartwarming letters from either bearers or recipients of the coveted olive branch of peace. Is not this a fine example of what just one person can do to make our world a better place?

Discord commits piracy upon our high spirits. Grievances unresolved rob us of precious time never to be relived in sweet harmony. Sadly, alienation and separation are intrinsic within the human condition. In other words, it is natural and human to hold a grudge. We humans can rise above this character flaw, however. We can choose to be *super*natural, to be *super*human, and forgive. Indeed, forgiving another person is a powerful act, and each of us possesses that very power! Be aware, however, that true forgiveness, like a real grudge, takes time.

While we are waiting and pondering forgiveness, it might help to read Luke 6:27–28, 36 (NCV):

> But I say to you who are listening, love your enemies. Do good to those who hate you, bless those who curse you, pray for those who are cruel to you... Show mercy just as your Father shows mercy.

Surely, Johnny Gruelle took this passage to heart as he guided the Raggedys throughout their numerous encounters with adversaries and came up perennially with happy endings for children.

In *The Paper Dragon*, he himself, a man of faith and the story's narrator, echoes the premise of the biblical text cited above: "For, it is best to be generous and unselfish, even to those who are unkind to us."[16] Wherever found, it is good advice. Forgive those who have wronged you in word and deed, and move forward. Embrace your own pain, for it can lead you to love.

Forgetting is another matter, a matter less significant than forgiving. Forget only if it is possible for you. Who knows? Perhaps *not* forgetting will prevent a similar hurtful situation from arising. Do remember the rage then and how it once ravaged your peace of mind. It is more important by far to forgive those who have hurt you and to learn from the experience of estrangement. You will be blessed, as peacemakers always are.

Shalom.

The last, best *Word* on Harmony is from 1 Peter 4:7–8 (NCV):

> The time is near when all things will end. So, think clearly and control yourselves so you will be able to pray. Most importantly, love each other deeply, because love will cause people to forgive each other for many sins.

Thomas

Thomas climbed out of bed and kissed Raggedy Ann on her painted cheek and smoothed her yarn hair from her rag forehead.[1]

—*Raggedy Ann Stories*, 1918

Raggedy Ann does a lot of falling. It's not that she is clumsy, mind you. Rather, the scripts of her adventures just call for much head-over-heeling. In one book alone, she goes "blumpity, blump" and varies her landings in a clothes hamper, a chicken yard, a tree limb, soft grass, mud, a paint bucket, and a brook! Furthermore, the method of choice for both Ann and Andy to descend a flight of stairs is throwing themselves down the steps, turning over and over as they fall, and landing in a heap at the bottom. "'Didn't hurt me a speck!' laughed Raggedy Ann,"[2] on one tumbling occasion (*Raggedy Ann and Andy and the Camel with the Wrinkled Knees*, 1924). She really does not seem to mind;

for Ann's sunny, happy, painted-on smile always remains before, during, and after her fall.

As far as I can read, though, Raggedy Ann never experienced the greatest falling adventure of all. She never did *fall* in *love*. She never even came close, even though a Mister Minky did try to steal her heart once upon a time (however, that is another story entirely). Then there was the little Brownie who planted a kiss on her cheek, but that amounted to nothing more than a freckle (*Raggedy Ann's Wishing Pebble*, 1925). Maybe she was just too old to bother. They say that it is never too late to fall in love; but just how old was she anyway in 1918, when we first met her in *Raggedy Ann Stories*? A very good source reports, "Even Raggedy Ann, with all her wisdom, did not really know how long Raggedy Andy and she had been rag dolls"[3] (*Raggedy Andy Stories*, 1920). Way to go, Ann! Keep 'em guessing!

Ironically, our "ageless" heroine has been surrounded by romance virtually all the time. Such is the artistic genre, in the broadest sense, used by Johnny Gruelle to depict Raggedy Ann's many adventures in words and pictures. Romanticism per se is characterized by a preoccupation with love or by the idealization of love. Furthermore, such writings and drawings emphasize imagination, emotion, and introspection; and they often celebrate nature, commoners, and freedom of spirit. Her spreading brotherly love among creatures great and small in the Deep Deep Woods makes Raggedy Ann a romantic heroine, to be sure. However, with no object of her affections, she remains unromantically inclined throughout her many adventures.

Just for comparison's sake, there is, nevertheless, another literary rag doll who was not so unlucky in love. She is the creation of noted American poet Carl Sandburg and appears in his whimsical collection for children called *Rootabaga Stories*, first published in 1922. This doll's love story is called "The Wedding Procession of the Rag Doll and the Broom Handle and Who Was in It." Wishing not to spoil the fun for anyone who has yet to enjoy Sandburg's account of true love in dolldom, I will only say that the Rag Doll chose the Broom Handle because he "fixed her eyes." Isn't that always the way!

Yes, this falling-in-love experience often starts with a mere glance in the right direction. Progressively, love's eager beginners find pleasure in just looking at each other. They then feed the feeling by seeing each other as much as possible. The eyes have it, that first go at love. Then it is the heart's turn next. Ultimately, true lovers must contend with the impossibility of separation, wherein the heart still feels but the eyes no longer see.

A remarkable and memorable fictional testament to love's enduring miracle lies within the pages of *The Notebook* (1996), a short but powerful first novel by Nicholas Sparks. A highly gifted southern writer, Sparks has based this work upon the unique lives and abiding true love of his wife's grandparents, and it is touching to the core. If you haven't done so already, I hope you will open your heart to all the other simple but poignant words that follow these in *The Notebook*:

> I am nothing special; of this I am sure. I am a common man with common thoughts, and I've led a common life. There are no monuments dedicated to me and my name will soon be forgotten, but I've loved another with all my heart and soul, and to me this has always been enough.[4]

Wonder why this phenomenon is tagged falling *in* love anyway? Somehow, the very idea of falling into anything connotes messy discomfort, akin to that of Raggedy Ann when she falls in the mud or into a paint bucket. Perhaps the phrase itself is one huge syntactic omen that has been ignored by mankind (and womankind) for centuries. Could it be that real-for-sure guys and dolls have been tumbling lickety-split into a pit of passion that is destined to become a pit of despair for most of them? Yes. Say today's excessively high divorce rate and domestic violence statistics.

"To be in love is merely to be in a state of perceptual anesthesia,"[5] penned H. L. Mencken. Problems, even separation and divorce, too often result when this infatuation wears off, when one's mate emerges as something other than a god or goddess. The marriage relationship, especially, works when partners fall in love over and over again—with each other.

It is necessary to *repeat* the falling-in-love experience because of its inherent finiteness. That euphoric feeling is not supposed to last. The orange blossoms do fade; the champagne does flatten. It is only natural with the passing of time. Moreover, vanishing the mist of infatuation clears the way for the real thing, if such is meant to be. The nitty-gritty of love is the reality of two people sharing a microcosm, their own little world, while continuing in, contributing to, and contending with the larger world around them. Where once there was but one, now there are two people who have chosen to live and grow together. This is love.

Unlike infatuation, real love is not temporary. It is also not easy. Nurturing the beloved requires putting someone else first. "It is only by forgetting yourself that you draw near to God," wrote Henry David Thoreau. Hence, the reciprocal giving and caring inherent in real love result in growth that is spiritual, as well as emotional and physical. In his best-selling book, *The Road Less Traveled* (Simon and Schuster, 1989), M. Scott Peck asserts the following:

> The essence of the phenomenon of falling in love is a sudden collapse of a section of an individual's ego boundaries, permitting one to merge his or her identity with that of another person[6]... Love's disillusionment occurs when these ego boundaries snap back into place. Real love is a *permanently* enlarging experience; falling in love is not.[7]

At one time, my local newspaper saluted couples celebrating fifty or more years of marriage. Each article included pictures of the pair as they were then, on their wedding day, and at the time of the article's publication. It indicated their respective careers before retirement and listed the names of their children. The article itself was brief, but the smiling then-and-now faces spoke volumes to the careful observer. Invariably, the young newlyweds' eyes appeared wide with anticipation, hope, and the promise of every dream being realized. Dimmed by age, these same eyes admitted to commitment, compromise, and courage in the face of life's realities.

Unsurprisingly, many of the men as bridegrooms wore, not tuxedos, but military uniforms. One imagines that they and their respective brides had become pitifully privy to the meaning of the adage, "War is hell." Undoubtedly, for them the pain of extended separation had both heightened and hindered the myriad other adjustments faced by all who marry.

On the other hand, perhaps the distance and danger imposed by war had so strengthened these lovers' bonds that complexities on the home front paled in comparison, as their years together unfolded. The grace of God and these couples' own ability to cope and to care whispered loudly their "secret" to such a long and happy coexistence. These golden-anniversary celebrants and others like them are very special and certainly worthy of public accolades.

My own parents appeared in this feature in 1983, their fiftieth year together. My four siblings and I further honored them with the traditional formal reception and a Caribbean cruise. On their sixty-first anniversary, in 1994, they gave us something. We got the chance to see in slow motion the beautiful bond that existed between our mother and dad. I say in slow motion because fate decreed that we all put aside our separate schedules and convene for nine long hours for this event. Having slipped on an acorn in her own front yard, my eighty-year-old mother underwent surgery on the anniversary day itself to replace her shattered left shoulder. Waiting it out with Daddy, who at eighty-one was amazingly agile and alert, we downed bad decaf and shared good stories, as the clock ticked and the surgeon labored.

That day, Daddy's random recollections to us about "Mother" (his home-front reference to her always—his own mother having been "Mama") extolled the order and the structure that she had wrought in his life and ours over the years. We offspring fully understood his points, readily acquiescing in most instances and freely contributing remembrances of our own, albeit with embarrassment at times. Collectively, we concluded that our mother's influence had been a quiet, almost imperceptible, influence for which each of us is all the better. Someone has aptly said, "A mother's love is love you never outgrow." It is such an integral part of what we become; it never leaves us.

In the sterile surroundings of that hospital, an infectious sense of belonging crept into my own heart. I realized that my four siblings and I are beloved entities in a real family, products of a loving marital union that had withstood the test of time. What a wonderful realization!

I distinctly recall thinking of O. Henry's beautiful Victorian short story, "The Gift of the Magi," at some point during that day's discussion. You remember, don't you? Della sells her long hair, her most prized possession, to enable her to buy a Christmas gift for her husband, Jim. It is a new chain for the gold watch that he so treasures. On Christmas morning, Della discovers that his gift to her is equally selfless; for Jim had sold his coveted watch in order to buy tortoise-shell combs for his beloved's long hair!

Real love is so predictably reciprocal. Hearing Daddy speak lovingly and unselfishly of Mother, giving her accolades so freely, I knew that she would, likewise, have credited him for his own strength and care as a husband and father. I would have to agree with her. His too had been a quiet, almost imperceptible, influence upon the lives of us children.

One year together, ten years, twenty-five, fifty years, and beyond… They are all amassed just one day at a time, aren't they? Caring couples—ever mindful of their vows to love, honor, and cherish—display mutual respect on a day-to-day basis. The essence of their togetherness is its quality rather than the quantity of its days. This day, they relish simple joys; that day, they endured some heart-wrenching trial. Another time, they celebrated a mammoth victory while daily confronting nagging frustrations and disappointments. The late Helen Steiner Rice penned this simply beautiful poetic summary in "The Meaning of True Love":

> It is sharing and caring,
> Giving and forgiving,
> Loving and being loved,
> Walking hand in hand,
> Talking heart to heart,

> Seeing through each other's eyes,
> Laughing together,
> Weeping together,
> Praying together,
> And always trusting
> And believing
> And thanking God
> For each other…
> For love that is shared
> is a beautiful thing—
> It enriches the soul
> And makes the heart sing![8] (from *Showers of Blessings*, 1980)

The most important person is the other person in a good relationship. Individuals who desire a lasting union put themselves last in a trinity, which they and their mates share with a Higher Power. Selflessness reigns supreme, to put it simply.

Far more complicated is an abusive relationship. Domestic violence, though complex in cause and effect, has long been an ordinary thing for the American family. It is extraordinary now only in its openness, a welcome by-product of the women's rights movement. Old English law and early American courts ruled that a husband might take a stick to his wife so long as the stick was not thicker than his thumb. This "rule of thumb" thus entered the language and fast became an ordinary, everyday phrase in speech.

Indeed, love gone bad is a reality—a distressing, often debilitating, ordinary, everyday reality. Hearing accounts of battered spouses always reminds me of a line from one of those famous 1960s anti-war songs: "Do it in the name of Jesus!" Hit her (or him) in the name of love? I don't think so. The touch of love should be tender and trusting, never traumatic.

Falling in love, then, takes courage. All colors of courage. The fiery reds of passion rage until they become but a glowing ember or else burn themselves out entirely. At times, the blacks and blues of violence and despair bleed unmercifully together. Often, the blues go it alone. Yellow cowardice lies in wait on the palette of emotions until it is needed for muting. It is very true: there are both physical and emotional risks involved in sharing feelings. No one has yet figured out how to remove the danger from human relationships.

Incredibly, however, our own little Raggedy Ann comes powerfully close to the solution in espousing the following precept: "Unhappiness can never creep in when hearts are filled with the sunshine of unselfish love"[9] (*The Paper Dragon*, 1926). That wonderful advice bears reiterating, this time in the words of Raggedy Ann's creator, Johnny Gruelle: "As you must surely know, they who are the most unselfish are the ones who gain the greatest joy"[10] (*Raggedy Andy Stories*, 1920).

The subject of physical abuse must understandably be presented delicately in children's literature. Johnny Gruelle had the most gifted manner of portraying despicable deeds to his young readers. To injure any living creature needlessly is not right. Those in a position to help the afflicted one should do so. Gruelle conveys these very admonitions through a doll nursery incident involving a hapless, errant Mamma mouse; the villainous cat Boots; and compassionate Raggedy Ann. Here is a part of what he wrote in *Raggedy Ann Stories* (1918):

> Boots would let the little Mamma mouse run a piece, then she would catch it again and box it about between her paws.
>
> This she did until the poor little Mamma mouse grew so tired it could scarcely run away from Boots.
>
> Boots would let it get almost to the hole in the wall before she would catch it, for she knew it would not escape her.
>
> As she watched the little mouse crawling towards the hole scarcely able to move, Raggedy Ann could not keep the tears from her shoe-button eyes.
>
> Finally, as Boots started to spring after the little mouse again, Raggedy Ann threw her arms around the kitten's neck. "Run Mamma mouse!" Raggedy Ann cried, as Boots whirled her over and over.
>
> Uncle Clem ran and pushed the Mamma mouse into the hole, and she was gone.[11]

Sadly, there will always be failures of love in the face of willfulness and spite. Kindness and intelligence have proven to be inadequate weapons against the villain selfishness time after time in one-on-one relationships. The best defense is a human spirit that will not be squashed, a sense of dignity that can lift the abused high above and far beyond the strife. "To look up is joy," taught Confucius. Remain optimistic, and never stop believing in yourself and your worth. After a bad fall, it is only natural to look upward and grasp an extended hand for assistance. More often than not, it will be there.

It surprises no one, I'm sure, to conclude with me that being romantically involved is a far more complicated issue than being just a plain romantic. Intimately sharing one's life has got to be more than a picnic in the park. Picnics are good, though. We all should find the time to enjoy more of them in this fast-paced world. Today, more than ever, we need to be true romantics, whether we are romantically "involved" or not.

Inserting a few simple pleasures within our hectic lifestyles can make all the difference in the quality of our days. For instance, grow your *own* tomatoes, for a change. They smell like no store-bought ones ever could! Surprise a friend or relative with a just-to-catch-up call. Put flowers on your dining table—even better, *grow* the flowers to put on your dining table! Being a romantic is easy and important. It is living simply and simply living. Every day.

Finally, a much lighter note "rounds out" this discussion of tumbling into love. You may recall when a national pizza chain chose lyrics from a familiar love song to tout its product on the airwaves: "Falling in love again… What am I to do?" crooned the smooth-voiced background balladeer amid pizza lovers' ecstatic sighs over melted mozzarella. Leave it to ad men to hustle and harness the most powerful magic in the universe to push pepperoni!

As for the rest of us, we too had better hurry—especially those who, like Raggedy Ann, have never fallen in love. Like Ann, also, we are not getting any younger. What are you waiting for? The pizza's getting cold! And oh, yes, be *very* sure to spread a red-checked tablecloth, on the floor maybe, and turn on background Pavarotti. I can guarantee that your pizza will taste even better; and someone will be impressed, even if you are dining alone! *Ciao*!

The last, best *Word* on Romance is from 1 Corinthians 13:4–8 (NCV):

> Love is patient and kind. Love is not jealous; it does not brag, and it is not proud. Love is not rude, is not selfish, and does not get upset with others. Love does not count up wrongs that have been done. Love takes no pleasure in evil but rejoices in the truth. Love patiently accepts all things. It always trusts, always hopes, and always endures. Love never ends.

Percy the Policeman

> I start to draw a great big picture jam packed with dozens of characters doing this-and-that, going which-way and what-way... Often I say to myself I shouldn't try this sort of thing. No one can do it properly but the master of uncluttered clutter, Mr. Johnny Gruelle.[1]
>
> —Dr. Seuss (Theodor S. Geisel), 1990

I dearly love my Raggedy room! This, of course, is the home headquarters for my own Raggedy Ann collection. It is a third bedroom that once served as safe haven to an offspring who has now sprung off on her own. The room is not a large one, measuring only inches more than ten by twelve feet. It has one standard-size window and a closet with double louver doors. Like all other painted surfaces in my home, the walls are off-white. As abysmally uninteresting as it may sound, this absence of color provides a perfect backdrop for the vivid reds and blues that predominate in Raggedy items.

These bright colors, along with welcoming smiles from the many Raggedy Ann and Raggedy Andy dolls, transform this collectibles site into a sweet therapy suite. There is just something about those Raggedy smiles! Invariably, the space they inhabit, especially *en masse*, will literally exude happiness and contentment. I find that, regardless of the weather, here for me is a place of perennial warmth and sunshine. It becomes an oasis of comfort when stress parches my being.

Lying down with a problem on the double bed therein, I am the only one to arise later on, refreshed. In its present location, this bed has afforded rest to far more of my concerns than to my company, I might add. However, my visiting stepson, sleeping there once due to lack of another space (when the guest room too was in use), related the next morning his dream of having been chased incessantly by lots of monster moppets, all with red yarn hair. The guy is forty-something and still is such a kidder! (Uh, I think.)

What my stepson really bedded down with in the Raggedy room is "organized clutter." It was nothing for him to fear but something for me to justify, perhaps. Antithetical in name only, organized clutter is a refreshing approach to decorating, which is akin somewhat to eclecticism but more challenging in its very density. Trust me. We collectors know all about density!

In truth, just navigating within these four walls is a feat, mainly because of the little floor space now left for feet! There's none right for feet, either! (Excuse the pun, please. Wordplay fascinates me, and I just can't help myself sometimes. I really think it has gotten worse since dear Dr. Seuss died. Go figure.) All space is fair game when accommodating a collection in the organized-clutter motif. The floor is really prime territory, and I have never regretted subordinating walking to displaying there. I just ask visitors to step gingerly as they might in either a minefield or a chicken yard. Most seem to catch on quite fast.

I have found that certain ones among my dolls actually prefer sitting on the floor. One such grouping is the nine-member clan of Knickerbocker Anns, ranging from forty to twelve inches in size. You have heard of "mother-daughter dresses," I am sure. Well, these sweet things, gathered in salute to generations of family, are all arrayed exactly alike in great-grandmother, grandmother, mother, daughter, stepdaughter, sister, aunt, niece, and cousin floral dresses!

They huddle contentedly, larger dolls snuggling smaller ones in their laps. (Do I hear a soft lullaby?) Favorite companions face one another, sitting closely and smiling broadly. (Was that a giggle?) A reader within the group but still alone in smiling solitude leans back and props her Golden Book on upswept knees. (Sigh.) It's a reunion of Raggedys! I wonder where they have stashed the fried chicken and potato salad…

Moving on up, those white walls of mine got covered faster than the Raggedys can tumble out a window. Believe me. When a collector of anything hangable starts hanging, blank walls are history! Moreover, we lovers of Raggedy especially can find pictures, prints, plates, and plaques galore. Puzzles too are at their beautiful best when put together and framed. One must remember, though, to keep some sort of method to the madness of wall hanging; otherwise, the result will not be the desired organized clutter.

With an entire room at a collector's disposal, it works best, I believe, to consider each of the four walls as a separate entity. Then, as they say, "Plan your work, and work your plan." Having decided which treasures are destined for a particular space, you should then project (imagine the results), prepare (assemble necessary tools), and proceed (go for it!).

My own Raggedy room has but one unbroken wall, and I wanted to make optimal use of it. The affordable purchase and easy installation of pre-cut and pre-painted shelving units, with accompanying standards and brackets, were the easy solutions. Centered against that ten-foot wall is the headboard of the bed, flanked by dissimilar tables. (Believing that they suggest timidity in decorating, I avoid suites or matched sets of furniture.) Also, I desired to keep in place, centered above the bed, a treasured signed and numbered Bob Timberlake print called *Friends*, which I proudly own.

It is one of three rendered over as many years by this noted North Carolina artist who used the Raggedys as subjects. Each one is precious in more ways than one. Measuring nineteen by twenty-four inches framed, it had already established itself as the room's focal point. It was there to stay! The new shelving design then had both to accommodate and complement this work of art.

Divide and conquer! Now, "framing" the print (on two sides, at least) are six separate shelves, each one eight inches wide and one-half inch thick. They are placed three per side, flush against the intersecting walls, in graduated lengths of four, three, and two feet from the top down. Making room for the Timberlake, I could have used all four-feet pieces of shelving instead of the shorter ones, thereby gaining an additional six feet of display space. I really would have relished the extra shelf space; for a collector can never have enough, you know. However, in my mind's eye, during my projection of the overall design, this combination of lengths seemed a way to "have my cake and eat it too." That is, I would get not the maximum but certainly ample shelf space while yet allowing the uncrowded artwork to take center stage, as it should.

The first shelf on each side is fourteen inches from the ceiling, a placement that puts the two shelves nine inches above the print. This expanse plus the two horizontal feet left between the long shelves (also directly above the print) yields no conflict. *Friends* can breathe! Completing the design on both sides, eleven inches down from the first, is the second shelf. It is followed by the third, spaced another eleven inches underneath. This unusual arrangement affords me a total of eighteen feet of commanding display area for unique acquisitions. Additionally, *Friends* remains intact in its place of honor—not depreciated in the least but rather enhanced now (and entranced) by collectible "friends" of its own.

The very first friends to scale the new heights were Raggedy Ann and Andy themselves disguised as ceramic cookie jars (MacMillan, 1993). Perched one to each side, they seem to have surely found their niche. In truth, these large containers are the reason those first shelves had to be fourteen inches from the ceiling. Not only do they show well from afar, but wee visitors cannot be tempted to lift the fragile lids in search of cookies!

Another rarer object of collectible interest that nestles on high is The Raggedy Ann and Andy Railroad Picture Puzzles (Milton Bradley, 1944). The original, well-preserved box, which is colorful and large, epitomizes nicely my penchant for earlier Raggedy memorabilia. All right, I admit to having put it up there just to flaunt it, but it was not without good reason. The location in my room is not the only thing "high" about this item!

Needless to say, the strategic placement of but three items, valuable or not, still leaves an abundance of space to fill on six shelves. Collectors everywhere would quickly agree with me that such is *no problem*. I have probably enjoyed most the versatility afforded by the shelf unit's design. Unlike the wall displays, collectibles on the shelves are easily interchanged on a whim, after a haul, or for a special occasion.

For the Christmas season and Valentine's Day, for example, I group holiday items for a really good seasonal show, albeit temporary. Also, my several first edition books by Johnny Gruelle are an endless source of pride for me. Hence, Volland favorites, like *Beloved Belindy* (1926) and *Raggedy Ann and Andy and the Camel with the Wrinkled Knees* (1924), get highlighted often. Wistfully, I still await the day when I can place these books' first edition namesake dolls alongside them on the shelf!

While I have you smiling over the aforementioned "high" improbability, I must mention something else that many collectors, myself included, are fond of doing just to bring a smile: it is having creative fun as we display our treasures, doing something that is fancifully unique—the use of whimsy! For instance, the tin doors of an old pie safe in my collectibles showroom swing wide permanently to display a myriad of Raggedy dolls and dishes. Its only drawer, left ajar, reveals colorful Raggedy linens: freshly laundered and folded sheets, towels and napkins ready for use. Eight tiny beanbag dolls playfully "climb" an elf ladder every which way but loose! Spaced ever so symmetrically, Raggedy limited-edition annual plates in porcelain (Schmid, 1970s) surround an heirloom wall mirror and become a feast for the eyes.

A Georgene, who arrived with no clothes, has the situation remedied by lounging in a sand bucket and is now sporting a tiny T-shirt that proclaims my sentiments exactly, "I LOVE HILTON HEAD." Is there any more perfect place for Raggedy Ann bedroom slippers (MacMillan Inc., 1988) than on a little heart-shaped braided rug beside the bed? Finally, at the flip of a switch, the Raggedy gramophone (Vanity Fair, 1974), never without a record on its turntable, fills the room with sunny songs. It is so easy and important to have tangible reminders that being a collector is fun!

As I have tried to show, in addition to bringing pleasure, being a collector of anything also means being a maker of decisions, not the least of which is *where* and *how* to display one's treasures. Raggedy things vary so much in shape and size, presenting a greater display problem than, say, thimbles, which are predictably compact and uniform. Besides the dolls themselves being in several sizes, there are available to collectors numerous Raggedy books and puzzles; ceramic figures, plates, and planters; lamps; bed linens; phonographs and records; wall plaques and prints; ornaments; and, oh, so much more! Why, there must be everything Raggedy but a kitchen sink.

Wait a minute. What am I saying? There *is* a Raggedy kitchen sink! It's by Hasbro (1978 vintage); and it holds and drains real-for-sure water and has a curtained window above it, complete with a sunny view! Really lucky collectors wind up with the matching stove and refrigerator as well. Hey, just call me a really lucky collector! My set is mint, pre-owned by a terribly tidy tiny tot who kept a spotless playhouse kitchen…at least, that's what I have surmised. The best part is that all three pieces (without a spot) were located and purchased (in the same spot) and presented to me as a gift by a dear friend.

Whenever this "friend" hankers for a cheap thrill, she relates once more to me how she first found the Hasbro set, immediately deemed it too unwieldy for words and for hauling in her compact car, and eventually left the consignment store *without* it. Just the thought still makes me turn pale and gasp for air, and she knows it. Some friend, huh? At any rate, she had driven away just far enough to ponder how I had not laughed when everyone else did at some really important events in her life. Like when she chose to sprinkle her dead dog's ashes under his "favorite bush" in her yard, or the time she discovered that the coiled obstruction in her car's engine had crawled on its belly to get there.

The important part, however, is that she cared enough to turn around and go that extra mile for me… Or was it four? (I should remember since she's told me often enough.) Oh, well, suffice to say that I *am* the proud owner of three Raggedy kitchen appliances by Hasbro! Raggedy Ann herself wants to have the last word here, I believe:

> And, as you surely must know, there is no feeling which brings as much true sunshine to our hearts as the happiness of honest, loving friendship.[2] (*Raggedy Ann's Wishing Pebble*, 1925)

Notwithstanding my kitchen sink, whimsically replete with "dirty" tin doll dishes (Bobbs-Merrill Co. Inc., 1972), a Raggedy room is in no way uniquely mine. I have met and read of many, many other collectors who boast of the same isolated, affectionately named location for their things. I say boast, for one should feel fortunate indeed to have a spare room to accommodate Raggedy Ann and all her many accoutrements.

The obvious alternative is giving the little redhead the run of the place one calls home. This pervasive approach is probably equally as popular among collectors in general as is the containment idea. I even know of those who have the special room to spare yet prefer to see their Raggedy paraphernalia throughout the entire house. So long as spouses, children, or pets living with the collector do not cry out in protest of territorial infringement, who am I to complain?

For me, however, having a finite space for my collectibles has an important advantage besides saving my marriage and promoting general tranquility. Remembering that space is at a premium makes me a more discerning, more discriminating shopper of my collectibles. To buy or not to buy a Raggedy item has been irrevocably decided, at times, by asking myself, "Do I want valuable space in my compact Raggedy room taken up by this object?" A negative answer or even a nagging doubt is all that I need to decline a frivolous purchase.

One collector's frivolity, though, is another's fanaticism. The very idea of collecting as a hobby seems to imply amassing objects without reservation, doesn't it? To date, the most prolific assemblage by which I have been awed is a Pennsylvania couple's *displayed* collection of over six thousand *sets* of salt and pepper shakers! Count 'em. That's more than twelve thousand pieces to keep dusted! The husband had built special floor-to-ceiling, very narrow shelving throughout the house to supplement the many glass-front cabinets devoted to the massive collection. When I jokingly asked the wife if she had a Raggedy Ann and Andy set, it took her less than one minute to recall just where it was housed.

An extensive accumulation seemingly endorses both the collector's proficiency in finding and dedication to preserving the cherished object. I daresay that few would agree with my own thinking that less is more in this regard. To own anything and everything bearing the Raggedy Ann image has never been my intent in fifteen years of collecting. In fact, I almost totally shun non-licensed items, which I have nicknamed "Raggedy wannabees." Moreover, I do not rush out to buy even licensed things from retailers, like expensive crib linens, for which I have absolutely no use. Rather, I avidly seek out the authorized commercial dolls, of course, and the books, especially the older examples of both. These two categories, dolls and books, are my personal passions as a lover of Raggedy Ann.

Furthermore, any miscellaneous Raggedy item of the 1940s or prior has special appeal to me, such as, the three Artograph puffy nursery prints, the earliest games by Milton Bradley, the 45 and 78 RPM Decca record albums, and the 1930s puzzles and paper dolls, to name a few. Part of the fascination with these older, more fragile collectibles is the sheer realization that they have survived at all. More importantly, however, concentrating upon these particular entities enables me to better appreciate Raggedy Ann's established eminence in Americana, as well as the artistic contributions of her creator, Johnny Gruelle.

Raggedy Ann entered the National Toy Hall of Fame in 2002. Raggedy Andy, often referred to as her brother, joined her in 2007. The dolls are reunited in this place of honor, where they surely belong—together, of course, for always.

"As American as Apple Pie" is the lettering emblazoned on a favorite Raggedy Ann nightshirt of mine. Truer words were never screen printed. Since her inception by Gruelle, in 1915, this little moppet has endured tenaciously. The only other imaginary character doll of the era that even comes close to matching Raggedy Ann in mass appeal is Rose O'Neill's Kewpie. Furthermore, regarding Ann's familiarity and her permanence, I have noticed an interesting dichotomy among non-collectors. The mere mention of the name Raggedy Ann prompts immediate recognition of her persona. Nevertheless, these same respondents are generally amazed to discover that the doll has been a successful commercial entity for over a *century*. My favorite means of keeping their mouths agape is to add quickly, "And would you believe that Raggedy Ann has also had her day in federal court [Gruelle v Goldman, 1937]!"

Most Raggedy Ann hobbyists of my acquaintance have this eerie, fiery-red glow in their eyes, right where the pupil ought to be. A reflection of Ann's red hair, it isn't. It is passion, pure and simple. It glows brightest, I have noticed, whenever they are in hot pursuit of an addition to their Raggedy collections. These devotees will endure five o'clock traffic, spousal ire, anxiety attacks, and every discomfort in between to become the proud owner of that must-have item. Moreover, isn't it wonderful that most of these hearts' desires are so affordable?

What's a mere $625 for a 1950s Georgene Ann, mint in the box? Who wouldn't lay down $975 in a solid red heartbeat for a Molly-E Ann wearing her original clothes? And Belindy is called beloved for a very good reason: there's a Volland out there somewhere for $3,500. Wow!

Are collectors frenzied fanatics? Some may be, perhaps, but not all are. The latter group of moderates, myself included, regularly tempers the fanciful enthusiasm with reality's constraints, especially money and time. I consider this exercise in self-control to be a refreshing extra benefit that I glean, a sort of collector's lagniappe, as they call a surprise bonus in New Orleans!

In my thinking, though, no one need ever apologize for being a passionate collector. Having a satisfying hobby or pastime of any sort is a life-enriching experience, and one cannot have too many of these. Every time I have occasion to visit a nursing home or other facility for the aged and infirm, it is the imposed and pervasive inactivity that saddens me so. I always depart with a renewed resolve to live more fully while I can.

Astrologically an Aries, I agree heartily with essayist John Burroughs's terse but true saying, "The secret of happiness is something to do." Raggedy Ann also knows the value of wisely using one's time: "Whenever a person has nothing to do, he becomes lazy and discontented,"[3] she warns in her *Golden Ring* (1961) adventure. The subject here is not necessarily one's work, not *that* kind of something to do, which actually may or may not bring pleasure. To get the most out of life, a person must have discovered ways to make living worthwhile, a task very separate from making a living. "Electrified leisure," I call it. I believe we all should fill spare moments and days with enriching experiences that can jolt meaning and depth into life and shock us out of inertia.

Here are a few of my own pleasurable pastimes besides collecting Raggedys: reading, creative writing, listening to music, dancing, traveling anywhere, visiting, being kind to strangers, exercising, learning anything new, volunteering, watching *Jeopardy*, recycling, loving, keeping a journal, gardening, planning surprises, taking a stand, laughing, taking pictures, contributing, phoning my siblings, worshipping, cooking for my family, dating my husband, challenging myself, walking, affirming others, playing cards, wrapping presents, attending meetings, petting somebody else's pets, shopping, eating chocolate, catching up with siblings, singing along to songs on the radio, decorating, hugging my grandchildren, cooking without recipes, teaching, chairing a project, corresponding, being with children, entertaining, refinishing furniture, making something from nothing, antiquing, coordinating outfits, serving others, remembering birthdays, clipping articles, styling my hair, completing crossword and jigsaw puzzles, lunching with friends, etcetera, etcetera. Boredom, begone!

Kids, teenagers especially, get into serious trouble sometimes because of sheer boredom. Their having nothing constructive to do can too easily result in something destructive to do. Youthful vandalism and petty theft serve as incubators for spawning career criminals, a cycle that has now become a sad sign of our times. Enraged, the public readily faults town councils and municipalities for their failure to provide wholesome activities and gathering places for restless adolescents. In truth, the very best of such efforts may prove to be "too little, too late" for most in this age group as they also must confront raging hormones and peer pressure.

The best solution to crimes by youth begins earlier (*much* earlier), and it is subtle, not sudden, I believe. Successful parenting demands, along with a myriad of other things, the early recognition of a child's skills and interests. Once acknowledged, they should no more readily be neglected than the young one's food and shelter. Agencies and individuals with nurturing opportunities, free and otherwise, abound in most cities and towns. Try to arrange for that budding athlete of yours to be on a team; seek out water for that swimmer or ice for that figure skater. Attempt to do more for the littlest artist in residence than just hanging his work on the fridge. Direct the symphony in a young soul so that it becomes music to your ears someday. And books. *Please* don't forget books!

Reading is a passport to planning and dreaming. You read to the youngsters, and they read to you. Local libraries are superb sources of other free youth entertainment, such as puppet shows, films, and storytellers. The benefits of such exposure, effort, and sacrifice on the part of a child by his parent or guardian are goose-pimply wonderful to imagine! Furthermore, the odds are good that a caring person's leading a kindergartner or elementary student by the hand toward training for some wholesome activity will preclude a policeman's leading him away as a handcuffed teen to training school.

Ironically, as I write this discussion about collecting and doing more things, the Lenten season is in full swing. Traditionally, Lent is, in the Christian faith, an austere period, a time when the believer chooses to live more simply—without excess, luxury, or ease. Technically, it is an annual season of fasting and penitence that begins on Ash Wednesday and lasts forty weekdays until Easter. The word *Lent* itself is a variation of the Old English *lencten* used in reference to the lengthening of daylight hours as spring approaches.

The spring season that follows winter's seeming lifelessness is a time of welcome renewal and rebirth. Everything in nature appears fresh and new! We humans, desiring the same ambience for our indoor environs, participate in a ritual called spring cleaning. I am told by those who do it right that one not only washes windows, baseboards, and such during spring cleaning; but that it is also the proper time to ditch out, throw, or give away items no longer useful or needed. Well, now, I can rub elbows with Mr. Clean with the best of them; but that part about tossing out is just plain not for me.

Do they really expect a teacher/collector, genus *pack ratus*, to throw out anything? The very idea… Besides being biologically impossible, it just goes against the grain. I have heard too many horror stories told by recanting tossers, wallowing in regret and pining for that long-lost tossee. Not me, no siree!

Adamant as I am about collecting and holding onto my things, I am far more agreeable to the idea of decluttering my life. The Lenten season, with its emphasis upon renascence, is really a good time of year for introspection and self-evaluation. Our lives, like our homes, do get cluttered. So much stuff is going on that purpose is lost, and basic emotional needs go unmet. The late Gilda Radner was exactly right, wasn't she? "It is *always* something!"

These many somethings pile up until, defensively, we say, "No more!" We then desire to be less involved, sadly, even with the things and people that really matter. Hence, Lent can become a reminder to get back to the heart of things. Yes, this means to become more spiritual, with prayer and devotions or in whatever context spirituality may be for you. It can be also a season of sharing yourself more freely with those you love. Welcome this time to *prioritize*.

To paraphrase Gilda, there *is* always something that we need most, something that will make us feel whole and complete and not segmented like so many separate pieces in a collector's trove. Could it be something as simple as the touch of a loving hand, a child's hug, the voice of a friend, or perhaps just the assurance that we are never alone? Why not collect all four of these, or similar precious things, in abundance?

Start today to seek out, find, identify, and recognize those very special things in your own life. Take care to shield them from the dust of apathy. Above all, *treasure* those people, as well as activities and, yes, even objects that make you happy and bring you joy. Hold them close to your heart, and never let them go.

The last, best *Word* on Precedence is from Matthew 6:19–21(NCV):

> Don't store treasures for yourselves here on earth where moths and rust will destroy them, and thieves can break in and steal them. But store your treasures in heaven where they cannot be destroyed by moths or rust and where thieves cannot break in and steal them. Your heart will be where your treasure is.

Eddie Elephant

Sitting in a comfortable chair was Marggy's Daddy. Marggy and her Mama ran to him and threw their arms about him, but he looked so surprised, everyone knew that Marggy's Daddy did not know Marggy and her Mama.

"Don't you recognize Marggy and her Mama?" Raggedy Ann asked.

"No! I cannot remember ever seeing them before!" Marggy's Daddy replied.[1]

—*The Paper Dragon: A Raggedy Ann Adventure*, 1926

She forgot to remember to bring Grace back inside. It was as simple as that. She never really meant for my doll's beautiful face to become crackled and lined like parched earth, or for its head's shiny ringlets to wind up a matted mess. The blue dress, once crisp and beribboned, was now a stained, stinking shroud. I repeat: my sister did *not* mean for this to happen. "Involuntary doll slaughter," the deed might be termed in playland jurisprudence. Ah, but one of life's great mysteries is a sibling's real intent in matters involving another sibling. The rub is "rivalry" or junior jealousy. You see, Claudia had a doll of her own—lots of them, in fact. What she did not have was a doll exactly like mine. This very fact, along with "I didn't *mean* to do it [of course]," became her defense at the ensuing parental inquisition.

Admittedly, I am not totally blameless in this particular doll disaster. I know now that I must have presented my six-year-old sister with a temptation she could not resist. I had proclaimed that I wanted to keep this doll forever, in her box, just as Santa had brought her to me. In my thinking, it was part of the impending and bittersweet rite of passage from my childhood into adolescence. In Claudia's thinking, that doll on a closet shelf was forbidden fruit that must be tasted!

The fall for Grace came sometime during the spring rains. Daddy found my dilapidated doll in an isolated exterior corner of our house, a perfect place to prey—uh, I mean, play—undetected. Only the doll's box, lightweight as a memory, remained. I threw the box away, but I have kept the doll's remembrance on the shelf of my childhood.

My forgetful sister has a counterpart in several of Johnny Gruelle's literary renditions of Raggedy Ann and her doll friends. The culprit is Marcella herself, the little girl who is the owner and caretaker, supposedly, of all the dolls in the nursery. Mistress Marcella breaches her duty of care over the dolls infrequently, however. It happens only when she is utterly distracted by some other, more glorious facet of being a child.

She forgot to remember to bring Raggedy Andy back inside. It was as simple as that. There he lay on the red sled in the snow while Marcella dashed inside for a donut, the distraction *de jour*. She never really meant for him to freeze "into one solid cake of ice all the way through," nor did she mean for him to wind up with a burst rag arm that she had "tried to limber up…before it had thawed out." The two were visiting Marcella's Gran'ma, who would discover Andy many hours later and declare, "He's frozen stiff as a board!" Gran'ma also had the idea to place Andy "in a pan of nice warm water until the icy cotton inside [him] had melted, and then [he] was hung up on a line above the kitchen stove"[2] (*Raggedy Andy Stories*, 1920). Do I even have to tell you that Raggedy Andy's eventual accounting to his doll friends in the nursery made all this sound more like an adventure than adversity? I don't think so!

What I do think is that all this talk about snow and remembering has suddenly reminded me of pansies. Yes, pansies. Early bloomers jolting our memories of spring, they can withstand the cold even though their fragile faces, slender stems, and tissue texture seem to admonish, "Handle with care!" Moreover, pansies do actually represent remembrance, you know. William Shakespeare said so, way back in the sixteenth century: "Pray you, love, remember, and there is pansies; that's for thoughts." (Willy did not mess up often, but this time, his grammar is atrocious!) Etymologically, the association between this flower and thoughtfulness has everything to do with the French *pensée*, meaning "thought."

So whenever you want another to know that you care, that you are thinking of her or him fondly, just remember the person in some way using pansies for inspiration. In season, gather and tie a small bunch with a narrow ribbon to take along when you visit. The sweet floral faces will continue the camaraderie long after you yourself have had to say goodbye. Present a few pansy seed packets as a token of love or appreciation. Write a note to a deserving someone on a card adorned artistically with colorful pansies that you have pressed. Let a nosegay of the silk variety be the finishing touch for a wrapped gift. Seemingly endless pansy presentation ideas result in a singular expression, which is that of care and concern. For this very reason, I'd bet my Molly-E that Raggedy Ann would choose pansies as her very favorite flower.

Inarguably, Raggedy Ann, unlike some of us, never forgets to be generous, kind, and caring toward others. She can still be included in the forgetfulness fold right along with the rest of us on at least one lesser count, though. Would you believe that she actually forgets the main reason for an important "in search of" adventure? It has happened to you and me a thousand times. You go to fetch something vital upstairs or somewhere; then *en route* you meet a distraction (say, doggy stuff on your bedroom carpet), and the matter at hand now changes entirely. In Ann's case, she and Raggedy Andy meet up with an old friend, and the three have a sort of subadventure. It's not quite as vivid as the hypothetical one above but exciting, nonetheless.

Little more than halfway through a ten-chapter episode, Andy casually mentions something that triggers Raggedy Ann's memory. She "clapped her hands to her mouth and exclaimed, 'Goodness gracious me! I forgot all about why we were searching for the little fat man. Don't you remember, Raggedy Andy? We wanted to ask him what he knew about the tree with the golden ring?'"[3] (*Raggedy Ann and the Golden Ring*, 1961). Soon back on track, the Raggedys proudly do accomplish their initial mission, despite a few more interruptions best categorized as dinky (in their case, Dinkie) and temporary.

Those same two adjectives, meaning insignificant and short-lived, might well be used to describe most of the nagging lapses in memory, the bouts of forgetfulness with which we humans must contend on a day-to-day basis. We start to introduce someone we have known forever and instantaneously forget his name. We leave the house, lock the door, and must return immediately for something we left behind. We return to a crowded lot unable to find the car that we had parked so carefully two hours before. We put valuables in such safe places that even we cannot unearth them later on. Distrusting our recall, we caution others to stop us if we have "told them this story before." Do not despair if you see yourself in these scenarios, for you are in good company.

Forgetfulness is no respecter of persons. Even the rich and famous forget at times most inappropriate. One evening while delivering a speech, Mark Twain forgot a word, strained his memory, faltered, then fumed at his own forgetfulness: "I'll forget the Lord's middle name sometime, right in the midst of a storm, when I need all the help I can get!" Another literary great, Robert Frost, was reciting one of his own famous poems at the inauguration ceremony of President John F. Kennedy. He promptly forgot a particular line and found himself being prompted by some perceptive onlooker, who was evidently a Frost fan!

It probably comes as no surprise to understand that both Twain and Frost were advanced in age when they experienced these embarrassing "Moments to Remember." (I can only dutifully beg their posthumous pardons for this intended musical pun and believe that at least one of them rather enjoyed it in between cigar puffs!) The momentary shame of forgetfulness for both men, as described above, was utterly human and totally inconsequential in light of their respective creative legacies.

These writers' great works are living proof that they did not, as some people do, merely obsess about the finiteness of their lives. Daily, they lived fully, always valuing the present, thus ensuring an enriched future life for themselves. Furthermore, the artistic genius of both men assured their immortality. As long as readers read, Mark Twain and Robert Frost will never be forgotten.

Fame has not everything to do with immortality, however. Simply being a loving grandparent, an inspiring teacher, or a good friend enables average people to touch those who will survive them. In these ways and in countless others, we can each strive to surpass our personal limitations and be remembered. An old poem that I first learned in eighth grade conveys beautifully the secret to living a life that matters. Here is the last verse of "Life's Mirror," by Madeline Bridges:

> For life is the mirror of king and slave—
> 'Tis just what we are and do
> Then give to the world the best you have,
> And the best will come back to you.[4]

More recently, on the occasion of his 2005 retirement, the departing chairman and CEO of a major southern corporation had this to say about successful living:

> Our legacy…will not rest with the new arts center or the new highway or the new skyscraper. The most important measure of our success will be how many broken spirits we heal and how many lives we touch.

I like that. I like that a lot.

A strong emphasis on the capacity to live fully in the here and now should not devalue the importance of the past. Certainly, we cannot *live* in the past. Yet just as importantly, we can and should *examine* our past and accept it as an integral part of our one and only life cycle. A favorite contemporary author, Barbara Kingsolver, writes in her fine novel *Animal Dreams*, "It's surprising how much of memory is built around things unnoticed at the time."[5]

These "things" somehow connected to us and, taken for granted in their moment, can in retrospect be given their proper due. Incidentally, did you know that even dolls possess memory? It must be so, for Johnny Gruelle relates the following about a doll that he knew quite well:

> Raggedy Andy did not speak (that is, through Marcella, as Raggedy Ann did in the doll nursery); he merely thought a great deal…
>
> He remembered many things that had happened years and years and years ago, when he and Raggedy Ann were quite young…
>
> The day might have passed very slowly had it not been for the happy memories which filled Raggedy Andy's cotton-stuffed head.[6] (*Raggedy Andy Stories*, 1920)

Likewise, we humans can, at will, take trips down memory lane and be nourished by the recollections of sights and smells, of people and places of our used-to-be. The senses, especially, can play a major role in resurrecting memories and feelings. How often it is that a specific sound, taste, sight or smell triggers thoughts of days that are gone but, seemingly, not forgotten. For example, wafting me right along with them, the cooking pungencies of certain vegetables invariably transport me back to elementary school.

My earliest lesson in advance planning was knowing at ten o'clock in geography class that I would *not* be eating turnip greens at noon in the basement cafeteria! Also, to this day, any sighting of blue polka dots or red pinstripes has teenage me dressed anew in heartfelt *haute couture*. That old Singer really sang as it cranked out designs by Mother! On another note, a train's wistful nighttime whistle is my cue to recall my favorite place of wide-eyed youthful dreams. Defying sleep, I lay in my girlhood bed on countless nights, making plans as numerous as the crossties of the railroad track visible from my window.

By simply reminiscing, then, we can be reunited at a moment's notice with our past and pack not a single bag. Who knows? We might even unload some weighty excess emotional baggage as we journey. "Happiness now is part of the sorrow then,"[7] wrote C. S. Lewis after his own painful evolving. Another acclaimed writer, Pearl S. Buck, who had numerous life experiences worth recalling, gave us this advice: "If you would understand today, you must search yesterday."

Admittedly, there are those for whom "the sorrow then" and the "searching of yesterday" are just too much to recall without skilled assistance. When such is the case, no shame exists in seeking help to harvest really bad seed. Indeed, do whatever is necessary to fallow stale emotions for renewal in the sunshine and fresh air of blessed deliverance!

The passage of time is a dependable and subtle balm for delivering humans from both emotional and physical pain. Almost miraculously, instances of joy amass in the psyche and linger there, as if to crowd out the hurt. I found this very idea presented most simply but masterfully within a short passage from Charles Frazier's highly acclaimed novel *Cold Mountain* (1997):

> He jerked when her finger first touched his wounds.
> "That's just pain," she said. "It goes eventually and when it's gone, there's no lasting memory. Not the worst of it, anyway. It fades. Our minds aren't made to hold on to the particulars of pain the way we do bliss. It's a gift God gives us, a sign of His care for us."[8]

Even with promised mitigation of past pain wrought by time, there are those whose yesterdays are so haunting that courage is yet needed to leave the familiar safety and take a backward look. Perhaps you have heard the story of the wartime prisoner who, day after day, clung tenaciously onto the bars of the single window in his dungeon, through which light streamed. One glorious day, a truce was declared, and his jailer left the door unlocked. He was free to go. However, the prisoner was too afraid to let go of the bars and leave the light that he had come to cherish. He was afraid to explore the dark, dark dungeon beyond his cell, thinking that he may never again see the beautiful light of day. The man died in a cell with an unlocked door!

Are you afraid to explore the darkness that is your past? Try not to be. Find the courage to act, to dispel any past fear that is robbing you of present joy. Once the journey is begun, we may venture as far into the recesses of remembrance as we desire. We should feel free to acknowledge in this backward look all the imperfections that we find within ourselves and others who have appeared in our life's drama. After all, many fine fabrics have natural flaws; we humans do too, in the tapestries that are our lives. Fortified by the experience of it all, at journey's end, we reappear from the past at the threshold of now. We are refreshed, resigned, and ready to resume living in the present. Recalling the past, a bittersweet task for most of us, has nonetheless a way of bringing us full circle, of making us whole. Try to remember. Try hard.

There are over five million Americans, at this writing, for whom trying hard to remember once-familiar people, places, and things is a daily uphill battle. Sadly, it is a battle they will lose. These people suffer from Alzheimer's disease—a degenerative disease that attacks the brain and results, first, in impaired memory; and then, wrong thinking and unpredictable behavior. Its cause is unknown, and there is no cure as of yet. Alzheimer's disease, named after the German doctor who identified it in 1907, is today the single most common cause of progressive intellectual decline, dementia, in adults.

Because the affliction direly affects the mind long before it debilitates the body, Alzheimer's patients linger in an ever-increasing swirl of forgetfulness of the familiar. One grieving husband remarked, "After forty-seven years of married life, now she doesn't even know me." People survive with this disease anywhere from three to more than twenty years (six or seven, on average). In time, they will not remember how to do necessary things, such as swallow, walk, or cover themselves up when cold. Reportedly, pneumonia and falls are common causes of eventual death.

The Alzheimer's Association provides the following as warning signs of the disease, most of which are related to memory:

- forgetting things more often and not recalling them later
- possibly preparing a meal and not only forgetting to serve it, but also forgetting that one actually made it
- forgetting simple words or substituting inappropriate words, making the statement incomprehensible
- becoming lost in one's own street, not knowing where he is, how he got there, or how to get back home
- dressing inappropriately, like wearing several shirts or blouses, perhaps
- forgetting completely what numbers are and what needs to be done with numbers in a particular situation, as in balancing a checkbook
- putting things in inappropriate places, such as an iron in the freezer or a wristwatch in the sugar bowl
- exhibiting rapid mood swings, from calm to tearful to angry, for no apparent reason
- experiencing drastic personality changes or becoming extremely confused, suspicious, or fearful
- becoming very passive and requiring cues and prompting to become involved

Once diagnosed, the disease and its unmistakable symptoms usher in many accompanying coping difficulties for other family members. By and large, the hardest thing is the relatives' no longer being recognized by the Alzheimer's patient—when in fact, they may be the spouse, sibling, child or grandchild. Experts advise relatives to learn as much as possible about Alzheimer's, to learn just what the disease does, so that they do not take resultant happenings so personally, especially the nonrecognition factor. Also, getting as many of the legal and financial aspects resolved in the early stages will be less stressful for all concerned. The most important, they admonish, is remembering to enjoy the good days and the good times with the afflicted loved one when they do come along in the course of the illness.[9]

Imagine, if you can, what it must be like for young people to witness these symptoms in someone they love, say, a grandfather who always took Chris fishing, a grandmother who helped Caitlin bake cookies. For parents who must contend with explaining Alzheimer's to a child, there are many good books available. I would like to recommend one in particular: *Grandpa Doesn't Know It's Me*, by Donna Guthrie, with illustrations by Katy K. Arnsteen (Human Sciences Press, Inc., 1986, in cooperation with the Alzheimer's Disease and Related Disorders Assoc., Inc.). It is beautiful in its very tenderness.

Of course, adult caregivers of loved ones with dementia face a myriad of spiritual, emotional, and practical challenges daily. These duties are highly stressful and unimaginable to others. Among the very best resources I have found in my own role as caregiver to my husband is Deborah Barr's beautiful devotional, *GRACE for the Unexpected Journey* (Moody Publishers, 2018). Its pages offer scriptural encouragement and practical advice from fellow travelers. Every page succeeds in ministering to specific needs of caregivers themselves, which are many and varied.

Finally, another bit of good news about a book! Marggy, Raggedy Ann's real-for-sure little girl friend in *The Paper Dragon* whom we mentioned in the beginning, is no longer distressed over her Daddy's condition at the end of Gruelle's story. While her Daddy is in a magic castle temporarily, some strange and unusual things happen to him, like, well, losing his memory. He is not ill, though; he has just been "magicked." Both Raggedys know all about magic, so they set about to find what is lost. After searching for a while,

> Raggedy Ann ran to the easy chair where they had first seen Marggy's Daddy; and there, sticking between the pages of a book to mark the place where he had been reading, was Marggy's Daddy's memory. Then, everyone was very happy, and Marggy's Daddy took them all on his lap and hugged them.[10]

What an unforgettable ending! Author Johnny Gruelle saw the importance of allowing even this fictional family to remember the good times and to concentrate upon the good days that lay ahead for them to share. Memory making…there is no better pastime! As author James M. Barrie penned, "God gave us memory so that we might have roses in December."[11] Let's take those wise words to heart and try to remember to make some wonderful memories of our own today and every day.

The last, best *Word* on Memory is from 2 Timothy 2:8 (NCV):

> Remember Jesus Christ, who was raised from the dead, who is from the family of David. This is the Good News I preach.

The Little Brown Bear

> For everyone knows, you can think ever so much better while eating cream puffs.[1]
>
> —*The Paper Dragon: A Raggedy Ann Adventure*, 1926

In order to gather food for thought while writing these essays, I have eagerly accompanied Raggedy Ann on adventure after adventure into the Deep Deep Woods and elsewhere. The journey has been a real picnic, let me tell you, a proverbial feast for my eyes and ears. She knows so many "characters," and they just seem to pop up from out of nowhere. I don't think I will ever forget this one particularly wild and crazy guy, a camel with very funny legs.

He could find his way anywhere at night but got lost in the light of day. He also ran backward a lot, and sometimes in circles, to get to where he was going. And oh, I must tell you about the two-headed dog guarding the inside of a castle that we visited! Believe me. You have not heard dog barks until you have heard *this* dog bark; for he barked very, very loudly. To our utter amazement, however, this ferocious-sounding animal turned out to be only six inches high! Talk about the bark being bigger than the bite. This critter must have coined the phrase. Needless to say, he was a magic dog. The Raggedys and I got "magicked" a great deal in our travels together, as you can probably imagine.

Personally, I would never have imagined that being with caring, kind, and innocent Raggedy Ann could prove hazardous to my health. Nevertheless, I found out the hard way that she is just too sweet for her own good (and mine). I think it all started with that reputed candy heart of hers. At any rate, our shared journey to hither and yon has been a piece of cake—a piece of cake, indeed…along with all the ice cream and lollipops and cookies and cupcakes and donuts and apple butter and ladyfingers and cream puffs that one could stomach. All of which will then be washed down with seemingly endless supplies of root beer, lemonade, and soda.

I know now why Raggedy Ann never told me to pack a lunch. Wherever we went, the goodies just grew wild on the likes of ice cream–cone bushes, root-beer trees with faucets, golden-biscuit trees, and in lollipop fields. Some treats miraculously appeared otherwise, as in apple butter–mud puddles and soda-water springs. Furthermore, I am here to tell you that they do not do veggies in the Deep Deep Woods! The closest we ever got to one was a dill pickle included in a lunch prepared for us by a good witch. She probably just got her magic "Will Tickle" charm crossed in the food formula somewhere and wound up with a happy unsweet accident that we could eat. That was also the only time I can remember eating pickles with ice cream without being pregnant. But when in Rome...

Now, if I can just get my tongue out of my cheek where it has been lodged like a jawbreaker during this entire introduction, I will surely be able to speak more seriously... There.

What in the world could Johnny Gruelle have been thinking to tempt children (and their parents) willfully with all these irresistible treats in story after story? First of all, he was just being true to his chosen genre: folklore, American style. In this medium per se, abundance in food just has to be included. Porridge, game, scones, and other such edibles smacked of the old European stories that had so heavily influenced Gruelle. He wanted something different on his own literary plate. Root beer, ham sandwiches, ice cream, and such provided the decidedly twentieth-century American taste that this writer craved. As for the plentiful servings, Gruelle, inadvertently or otherwise, was helping to boost the morale and raise the spirits of impoverished Americans.

Writing prolifically from the late 1920s to the early '30s, a period of national economic deprivation, he consistently used the themes of generosity, kindness, and thrift. These attributes, coupled with endless good things to eat within his stories' pages, were Gruelle's alms to the poor. They were nourishing symbols of hope for the future in the face of debilitating despair.

Now I think I'll have another jawbreaker.

It pleased both Raggedy Ann and me immensely to have Raggedy Andy join us for many of our adventurous jaunts. Long-standing friends, they complement each other's actions quite well and share the same ideals. Also, until a caring Mister Muskrat remedied the situation, the two rag dolls shared something, shall we say, less palatable as well. Neither of them could eat anything.

> "I wish that we could," Raggedy Ann sighed, "But you know we haven't any real, for-sure mouths like you folks and when we taste anything, it just runs and soaks in our rag faces!"[2] (*Raggedy Ann's Wishing Pebble*, 1926)

Using a large nail, their friend Mister Muskrat poked a hole right in the center of the Raggedys' mouths, a hole just large enough to accommodate a straw. Well, sir… Those two immediately commenced to compensate for lost time. They went from never having eaten anything to slurping fifteen ice cream sodas at one sitting! And how do the Raggedys spell *relief*? M-A-G-I-C, of course.

Gulp. My jawbreaker! I think I swallowed it! I'm serious!

Most likely, for us real-for-sure people, there is some diet plan out there with the word *magic* in its name. At last count, the number of weight loss concerns and wireless phone plans was about the same—a bunch. With nearly three in four Americans overweight, it would certainly appear that we now need, more than slightly, either dietary sleight of hand or change of heart. Based on a recent Harris

Poll, which surveyed 1,250 adults nationwide, 80 percent of Americans aged twenty-five and older are overweight: from 58 percent in 1993, to 64 percent in 2000, to 71 percent in 2005. It concluded further that 83 percent of American men are overweight and 72 percent of American women, with the proportion of overweight people increasing with age.[3]

Doctors distinguish between *overweight* and *obesity*. A person generally is not considered obese unless his or her weight is at least 20 percent higher than the recommended range based upon one's height and body frame. The past decade's obesity research declares that an estimated eighty million Americans are clinically obese; and nearly three out of four are overweight, including one out of every five teens.[4] According to the Surgeon General's Office, 300,000 deaths yearly are attributable to weight-related diseases, including diabetes, strokes, heart attacks, and certain cancers. A Harvard Medical School professor, Dr. JoAnn Mason, recently stated in an interview, "It won't be long before obesity surpasses cigarette smoking as a cause of death in this country."

This alarming epidemic is brought to you in part by the "magic" of technology. This is just my opinion; but such a pronouncement, for real, might well be accompanied by background musical strains of the beautiful ballad "Killing Me Softly." In other words, so many things that make life easier and more fun also promote obesity and overweight. Automation and convenience are, at once, things we live with and die from.

I have always thought that so-called convenience stores were so aptly named, for they do sell convenience. It is true that one can dash into one for a gallon of milk or a loaf of bread and be out in a flash. However, look how much more those items cost there than in a volume supermarket. One pays dearly for the commodity of convenience. Apply this last thought, if you will, to the high percentage of folks who would never, ever opt to use stairs when there is a perfectly good elevator or escalator available to them. Indeed, convenience is costly.

Another dear expenditure is health care in America, which now costs well over $3 billion a day. Is it not actually "sick care"? Could not the proverbial one ounce of prevention really and truly be worth a pound of cure in this regard? Published by Archives of Internal Medicine, recent findings by Kaiser Permanente (an Oakland, California, health provider), include the fact that health costs of their obese members are 44 percent higher than the average.[5] This is a staggering assessment. Lowering fat intake and exercising moderately are two panaceas available to all and are free for the taking. Moreover, what we do for ourselves to maintain good health is far more vital and timely and consistent than what any doctor can ever do for us.

Lame excuses for not exercising will probably make the whiner himself lame sooner or later. Contrastingly, the benefits of regular fitness activity are absolutely astounding! Try it. You will be amazed at your increased energy and efficiency and your reduced stress. The heart muscle will pump with far less effort; arteries will become clearer of fat deposits; blood pressure and blood sugar levels will be lower. Furthermore, exercising increases the flexibility in joints and the calcium content in bones. It slows the loss of muscle tissue, speeds up reaction time, and even helps to curb certain cancers.

Additionally, the latest good news is that fitness does not have to be fanatic. *Anything* you do that gets you up off the couch will prove beneficial, like doing the twist when you vacuum or washing the car yourself, for instance. And walk, walk, walk! Sweat and speed are unnecessary to reap benefits from walking. Tests have shown that fast walkers burn more calories while slower walkers burn more fat. You are a winner either way! It is important to understand, though, that immediate and drastic weight loss is not going to happen with exercise. It is diet plans that tout quick weight loss, but it is exercise that puts a person in control of his own body weight. Long-term, however, consistent activity could easily account for the devotee's weighing twenty to twenty-five pounds less for the rest of his or her life. Trimmed and toned—what a beautiful combination!

Today, because they never stray from their comfortable ways ever to exercise, 60 percent of Americans must be classified as sedentary. The President's Council on Sports, Fitness, and Nutrition (PCSFN) recommends thirty minutes of moderate activity five times a week. Once on the move, it is those in this very group who realize the greatest increase in health benefits, according to ongoing research at the Cooper Institute for Aerobic Research in Dallas, Texas. Another recent survey by the PCSFN has revealed an interesting dichotomy: the majority of the respondents who did not exercise said they did not have time, but those same respondents admitted to watching five to seven hours of television each week. There is something definitely wrong with this picture.

The Center for Science in the Public Interest puts the problem into even sharper focus. This consumer advocacy group has found television viewing time to be about four hours per day for the average American. Inarguably, television, along with the automobile (both as commonplace as dirt and just as affordable), are cornerstones of a comfortable lifestyle, with most modern families having more than one of each. We sit and watch; we sit and ride, for hours on end (no pun intended.) Moreover, seemingly as a general rule, while we are sitting (especially sitting and watching), we are also eating. Now, there are *three* things running like crazy: the TV, the car, and the calorie counter.

Do you eat to live or live to eat? This is one of those questions to which people know the answer the moment you enter a room. Those of us who eat to live use food to *nourish* our physical bodies and to impress our friends at our Christmas open house. Those who live to eat use food to *fill* their physical bodies and to assuage their hurt when no one shows up for their Christmas open house. The point, of course, is that food sometimes gets misused. It gets eaten for all the wrong reasons.

Food must hate that too—being abused. It hates being abused so much that it turns right around and abuses the abuser. The more food gets abused, the more it retaliates. It's a real Mexican standoff, or maybe Italian or Chinese, perhaps. Food abusers soon develop certain telltale signs. One is an unmistakable, kangaroo-like pouch filled with, not babies but blubber. They're certainly not moving like any kangaroo, though, due to overweight and clogged arteries and such. It's usually not a pretty sight.

As badly as it can do in its abusers, food fights fairly, generally living up to its sundry names. Fats, the real villains, are the ones to watch, which is not a simple task when we realize that there are actually a few good guys among the bad. Bad fatty acids are the biggest source of bad cholesterol (LDL), the reputed cause of heart disease. Labeled saturated, polyunsaturated, or hydrogenated fats, these come primarily from vegetable oils and animal foods, especially red meats, cheeses, ice cream, and whole milk. Include them respectfully in your diet, allowing them to represent no more than 6 percent of total calories consumed. (There are nine calories per gram of fat.)

So who are the "good-fat guys" that I alluded to earlier? Well, they also break down in our bodies to form cholesterol; but it's HDL, the okay kind. You see, we need *some* fat in our diet, just not an abundance of the bad kind, which clogs arteries. In fact, 20 to 30 percent of a day's calories can come from fat, hopefully with emphasis on the monounsaturated variety. Lean toward fruits, vegetables, whole-grain bread and cereals, fish, nuts, and canola or olive oil for seasoning. Also, read the fine print on food packaging. Often, that "fat-free" splashed onto the front boils down to mean that they are not charging you money for the fat.

Do not allow fatty foods to turn on you. Do not abuse them please, for you will not be able to hide what they will do to you in return. By the way, you will have a real fight on your hands with fats in any fast-food restaurant.

Trust me. You will not have it your way even when seated beneath golden arches.

I found myself on the dietary defensive more than once as I took part in Raggedy Ann's many adventures. The mere suggestion, albeit figurative, of all those enticing goodies too often triggered my appetite. Hence, "running" with the Raggedys for research, I also ran the risk of giving in to cravings prompted by Gruelle's abounding literary sweet treats. As we have seen, both the Raggedys were hopeless cases. Anyone who can make fifteen ice cream sodas disappear in one sitting has zero willpower! In truth, I'm afraid their love of sweets began innocently enough back in the doll nursery with Mistress Marcella's concoction of brown sugar and water—which she used quite often for medicine, tea, and/or soda water[6] (*Raggedy Andy Stories*, 1920).

Cravings can indeed be the result of childhood food associations, memories, cultural beliefs, traditions, or other powerful emotional cues. Some may be mere habits. Also, some really strange things with even stranger names (like endorphins, tryptophan, insulin, and serotonin, for example), all found within the body's chemistry, influence when and what we eat as well. What we eat, in turn, affects how we feel directly and indirectly. It stands to reason then that if something we ingest makes us feel better emotionally (i.e., less anxious or more exhilarated), we will not so readily cast it aside even if we know the food to be nonnutritious. The only true course of action with cravings then is to learn to work with them. Exercise some control.

Exercise indeed! Doing so regulates blood sugar levels and provides the pleasurable rush (from endorphins) that reduces stress. Decreased craving for sweets is automatic with a regular program of exercise, not to mention the weight maintenance! Another means of automatically curbing food desires is drinking lots of water, especially after dinner. You may think you want something sweet when in fact your body is thirsty after a long, hard day. Try it. And be sure to squeeze a small wedge of lemon into that healthy "toddy for your body"!

Do yourself the favor of starting the next day with a simple but nourishing breakfast of grains and fruit (one serving of each, at least). Skipping this important meal has your hungry self playing right into the hands of some non-nutritious craving later in the morning. Finally, work *with* your desire for sweets by actually satisfying the urge with a healthier alternative: one naturally sweet, perhaps, or certainly one that is low in fat. Fruits, fruit products, and non-fat yogurts figure in beautifully here. When you really love sweets, denial gives birth to binges. Maybe you can't just say no, but you can say *low*, as in low fat.

The only sweet that I must struggle to refuse is chocolate even though I willingly and religiously do without the divine stuff for the forty days of Lent. I began this practice in 1987, and that very first season of denial presented my willpower with its test of tests. Comparatively, every year since has been a piece of (non-chocolate) cake!

Vacationing in Hawaii that year for the first time, I quickly learned that the islands' most popular dessert, offered in every eating establishment worth its poi, was the infamous Hula Pie. It is a multilayered concoction, complete with nuts and cream, including every shade of chocolate imaginable, and assembled in a nutty (chocolate, of course) crust to die for! "Just put it out of your mind," I say to myself. Yeah, sure! Not thinking hula in Hawaii is like not thinking space on Mars. I endured an appetite ambush at every turn! It was awful. The really awful part—or perhaps *awe-ful,* as in "solemnly impressive"—is that to this day I have never tasted Hula Pie!

Its distinctive smell, color, and taste are about the only things good about chocolate, unfortunately. This sweet is a detrimentally delicious combination of sugar and fat, along with other compounds, including caffeine, phenylethylamine (PEA), and theobromine. If these latter three sound addictive, they are and highly so. Eating chocolate brings about a real pleasure unmatched by any other dietary indulgence. The more real chocolate we eat, the more we want. I am convinced that it was a hopeless chocoholic who first uttered, "The devil made me do it," while finishing off a five-pound box.

What's a health-conscious chocolate lover to do? Well, for starters, do not ever buy the tempting stuff in five-pound boxes, oversized bars, or other large quantities. Give your willpower a fighting chance, for goodness' sake! Satisfy your urge with a chocolate dessert after a nutritious meal. This is the "lesser of two evils" approach to eating chocolate. It's still just as bad for you, but you probably won't consume as much on a full stomach as you would on an empty one. What I often do is lightly dip fruit, especially banana slices, strawberries, and grapes, into low-fat chocolate syrup and tell myself that it's good for me. Well, it is good, and it is for me! Chocolate really is good. Let's just remember to be good to ourselves when enjoying it. I promise to try if you will.

Here is a statistic that may shock you: Today, the average American consumes almost 152 *pounds* of sugar in one year! Admittedly, that total is not for pure sugar alone, but rather it represents our intake of sugar in all its many forms and varieties.[7] Pure sugar consumption has actually dropped in recent decades, but don't applaud just yet. We may have jumped from the sweetener frying pan into the fructose fire. We now use more high-fructose corn syrup, with its rate of consumption having increased 250 percent in the past thirty years, according to the Department of Agriculture. The dubious credit goes to soda makers, who switched in the early 1980s because it was cheaper than sugar. A concentrated sweetener produced from cornstarch, high-fructose corn syrup is also found prolifically in cookies, syrup, jams, jellies, bread, canned juices, peanut butter, sweet pickles, sweetened teas, seltzers, and fruit drinks.

Read package labels as high-fructose corn syrup, if included, *must* be listed among the ingredients. It's the law. Remember too that the closer to the beginning of the list the sweetener is, the higher the concentration of it in the product. Awareness is all that is being advocated here, for the research on the impact of high-fructose corn syrup on health is ongoing. What is already known, however, is that it can further aggravate effects of an already nutrient-poor diet, most especially one lacking in chromium, magnesium, and copper.

There's something important regarding chromium, which is a mineral essential to the body's ability to use sugar: tests on those who heavily consume high-fructose corn syrup have revealed lowered levels of this element. This condition sets the stage for an increase in sugar, LDL cholesterol, and triglycerides in the blood—all of which are key risk factors for diabetes and heart disease.[8] The healthy course of action is fewer sweeteners of any kind in the diet and more whole-grain breads and cereals, along with fresh fruits and vegetables rich in these minerals.

I want to recommend a classic book if you will promise not to eat something bad for you while you read it. It is called *The Garden of Eating* by Jeremy Iggers (Basic Books, 1996). He expounds upon food as the unlikely nemesis of life in America, involving the startling contradiction between the prodigious bounty of this country's table and the unprecedented levels of anxiety and prevalence of eating disorders that we endure. Highly palatable reading, it will cause you to gain insight, so lap it up! A far more recent recommended read is the 2005 Pulitzer Prize commentary nominee Tommy Tomlinson's insightful memoir, *The Elephant in the Room* (Simon & Schuster, 2019). Honest and affecting to the core, it is a powerful must-read for food addicts seeking release from shame and self-consciousness.

In closing, I have a confession to make. Raggedy Ann would want me to be totally honest with you, so here goes. Out of necessity, I have had to write about food in this discourse with a certain clinical detachment. I have never dieted, yet I wear the same size four as I did decades ago. It's a metabolism thing, I suppose; for I can eat anything I want, but I am not passionate about food either. I can take meat or leave it; however, pork is definitely off my menu. My portions are usually small and my choices, generally healthy. I try to ingest nothing after nine o'clock at night, much less an entire meal. My favorite area of the supermarket is the produce section, and I never met a bread I didn't like. I respect and understand food. Acceptance and love, it isn't. I know this. Food is just food to me. I know that good food nourishes and bad food kills, slowly but surely. It's that simple to me.

As for exercise, I just do it, like brushing my teeth. It is part of my day, every day. Putting technology to work for me, I use a half-hour weekday toning, stretching, and low-impact aerobics workout program televised from beautiful Hawaii. For further activity, I love to dance, and all my shoes are made for walking (not just my boots!). Incidentally, here's something else Raggedy Ann would want me to mention for the children's sake. From the label "Kid Stuff" (product #5012) comes the delightful *Raggedy Ann and Andy Bend and Stretch: A Very Special Exercise Record for Children*. Let's get 'em started early on the road to healthy activity!

This personal credo of mine concerning exercise and food will be, most likely, for many others quite hard to swallow. I fully respect and understand their objection. However, I also understand the reality of a person's digging a grave with eating utensils. I have watched it happen to people that I love. This saddens me even though I know with certainty that it will never happen to me. Every person needs to reckon with exercise and food, fats and sugars, in his or her own way and time. A great percentage never will, though. They will continue to live as if it does not matter what they eat or how little they exercise.

There may be some merit in perceiving food choices as the final frontier of personal freedom. I wonder, though, is even *liberty* enough justification to commit suicide by ingestion? "I'll eat whatever I want even if it kills me" has a decidedly spiteful ring to it, doesn't it? What of eating and the *pursuit of happiness*? "I'll eat whatever I want and die happy." Well, all right, if you insist. But before you go—due to either liberty or the pursuit of happiness—pay homage please to *life*, the vital third member of this historical trilogy of life, liberty, and the pursuit of happiness. Notice that life is named *first* in the threesome. Only you can make the healthy food choices that will make your own life last. So please eat to live.

The last, best *Word* on Body Maintenance is from 1 Corinthians 6:19–20 (NCV):

> You should know that your body is a temple for the Holy Spirit who is in you. You have received the Holy Spirit from God. So, you do not belong to yourselves, because you were bought by God for a price. So, honor God with your bodies.

Sunny Bunny

Nature has such wonderful things to tell us in such beautiful ways, if we can only try to understand.[1]

—*Raggedy Ann and the Happy Meadow*, 1961

Okay, now, here's the plan: it's onto the windowsill, followed by a short but quiet drop to the roof, and an easy glide down the corner rainspout. Once on the ground, you should run straight for the hole in the orchard fence, where a tiny path leads to the deep, deep woods. You got that?

Such is the tried-and-true doll nursery escape plan used countless times by Raggedy Ann, whose runaway partner is most often Raggedy Andy. Although they all are privy to the plan, the other captive dolls are either less adventurous or more content to stay tucked in their beds (or perhaps both). Nonetheless, when the two Raggedys have endured an especially hard day in the playhouse with Marcella, they can hardly wait for nightfall to come and have for themselves a respite of a different kind.

In case you are now wondering, the "dark…does not make any difference to dolls. They, having sharp little eyes, are able to see in the dark as well as in the light"[2] (*Marcella*, 1929). And besides, the Deep Deep Woods are magical! It can be dark as pitch in the real world, but the sun yet shines down the tiny path beyond the orchard fence. Also, this hallowed Raggedy sanctuary is "filled with fairies 'n' everything,"[3] (*Raggedy Ann in the Deep Deep Woods*, 1930) as you can probably imagine. Or can you?

Johnny Gruelle, the real-for-sure person who created all of Marcella's nursery dolls in stories and pictures, certainly could. His very favorite artistic locale in book after book was a lovely, natural woodland setting densely populated by fairies, elves, and gnomes. Colorful creatures and cozy critters with alliterative names and altruistic natures assist the errant Raggedys in gently persuading boys and girls to do the right thing.

The author seemingly knew that not all other real-for-sure people could share his own close affinity for nature. He writes in *Raggedy Ann in the Deep Deep Woods*:

> I guess you have been out in the deep, deep woods, filled with fairies 'n' everything lots of times. And, if you have, then you know just how lovely everything is there. The great trees above your head whisper as you pass beneath… And although you hear the trees whisper to

each other, maybe you can not understand just what it is they say.

But with Raggedy Ann and Raggedy Andy it is different, for they know just what the trees are whispering about. They know just what the lovely birds are singing, and why the pretty flowers nod their heads to each other.[4]

In truth, however, Raggedy Ann and Andy did not always possess this heightened sensitivity for the things in nature. The change came about when they had the good fortune to befriend one Grampy Hoppytoad, who was all-knowing about the natural world. Why, he was the one who explained to them where a laugh goes when you cannot hear it anymore, as well as how the woodpeckers got their red heads! Are these eternal questions or what? Moreover, one fine day, their mentor and benefactor gave to each of the Raggedys a magic potion that forever altered their outlook on the woodlands and meadow where they loved to romp. Here is how the new and improved Raggedy Ann responded:

> When Raggedy Ann sat up, she gazed about her everywhere and breathed a long "Ohhh" of delight. The flowers looked more colorful than they had ever looked before. Even the grass was such a bright green that it made her shoe-button eyes want to blink. And the sunbeams falling

everywhere over the meadow shone like beams of gold. But best of all were the lovely, dainty fairyland creatures playing about in the meadow.

"Isn't it beautiful, Raggedy Andy?" Raggedy Ann whispered.

"Indeed, it is," Raggedy Andy quietly answered.[5] (*Raggedy Ann and the Happy Meadow*, 1961)

Now might be a very good time to tiptoe away from the awestruck Raggedys for a while and get our own breath of fresh air. I was just thinking more about this escaping thing and how really necessary it is for us real-for-sure people. We work hard. It's stressful, strenuous even for some. We play hard. It's fun but physically demanding. We love hard. It's why we're here, but it charges the emotions in more ways than one. The human body, mind, and soul are in constant need of replenishment. We all know this, and the smart ones among us do what we know we should. We eat right, exercise, get adequate sleep, and smile a lot. The ones who cannot or will not do these simple favors for themselves will probably not live to tell about it.

Let's get back to nature here, literally. What's in it, in nature, for us and our well-being? What can Mother Nature offer us that will save us from ourselves? The answer is *everything*. Fresh air and sunshine, ripe tomatoes and summer squash, beach sand and purple mountains, all readily come to my mind. However, these are certainly not favored by you if you freckle easily, think that squash should be squashed, and live hundreds of miles from the nearest ocean. The panacea that we humans seek then, this gift from the natural world, must be something far more universal, something far less subject to taste and distance and skin tone. That it certainly is.

Nature gives to us all the glorious gift of *order*. She has a plan, an *orderly* plan, unlike most of us who daily perform in that infamous "quiet desperation." Just look at the seasons! Like clockwork, winter becomes spring; spring yields to summer; and summer must, in turn, make way for fall. Nature's plan is a plan we can count on, a plan we can learn from. It is a plan that we are already a part of but from which, unfortunately, we too often depart as we live our lives. Take a moment to think about your life. Is it in any way hectic and chaotic? Are there things, large and small, that you do regularly that you feel are actually a waste of time? Could any of your tasks be delegated to another? Do you go too long without making time for yourself?

Who among us can truthfully answer no to *all* of these lifestyle questions and others in the same vein? The ill that plagues us all is *stress*. (You had that one figured, already, huh?) Unsurprisingly, medical research continues to establish a direct correlation between our physical well-being and stress, especially among working mothers. The gauge is the stress-response hormone called cortisol. Even though people's stress response is highly individual, excess stress generally yields excess cortisol, which is unhealthy for several vital reasons. Primarily, it suppresses the immune system, leaving us more vulnerable to infections and other diseases—even cancer. It also results in elevated cholesterol and blood pressure levels.

Ironically, if stress is all around us, its remedy surrounds us as well. It is right under our nose, above our head, under our feet, and by our side—in nature. "All that we see, everything that is growin' in the earth, is healing to the nation of any kind of disease," a local aged herbalist was fond of saying about the leaves, roots, and bark from which she would concoct natural remedies. Of course, these "secrets of the woods," as she called them, were intended for her treatment of physical afflictions.

In my thinking, however, her sage words about the power of the things in nature to heal can be applied to our emotional and spiritual wounds as well. Folk medicine today is an endangered species because too many people watched the practitioners but did not see; they heard their words but did not listen. Perhaps that is our problem with returning to nature for an emotional balm for stress. We do not listen for nature's promptings, and we simply cannot see the forest for the trees. "Come into the light of things," said William Wordsworth. "Let nature be your teacher."[6]

Appreciating nature and learning from her are one and the same thing, I believe. It can even be said to happen simultaneously. Hence, if we wish to profit from nature's bounty, we must commune with her at times, in some ways, and on some level that will give her the chance to speak to us and soothe our stressed spirits. Right now, let's choose something in nature and experience it together. Let's see which doors beyond the obvious will be opened to us. Since this was my idea, I get to choose, and I choose flowers!

Hold on, though, for there is absolutely no way that we can talk about flowers and not let Raggedy Ann in on the discussion. She is a real flower child if ever there were one. Why, every single one of her favorite dresses is flower-splashed! She also stops to touch and smell almost every blossom she sees during a nature romp with Andy. Here is one floral encounter from the pages of *Raggedy Ann and the Happy Meadow*:

> Raggedy Ann and Raggedy Andy noticed the pretty lilies and stopped to watch them bowing to one another. The soft, gentle breeze blew on them and made their green dresses rustle like Grandmother's old silken skirt. And the Raggedys could also hear a sound as of Fairies whispering.
>
> "How lovely the lilies are!" Raggedy Ann softly said. "They seem to make you want to be ever so quiet, as if you were trying to hear beautiful music coming from far, far away."
>
> "Indeed, the scent of the flowers is part of Nature's beauty," a tiny voice said to the Raggedy dolls. "Just as is the music of all the creatures…"
>
> "Yes… Truly, their perfume is the message that the flowers send to tell us of

Nature's great wonder and beauty. And what wonders and loveliness it would tell of if folks could only understand."[7]

Well, all I can say at this point is that little Raggedy Ann really knows how to pick her flowers! I myself could not have chosen one better than the lily upon which to begin our reflection on the inherent message of flowers. And the lily is just what the doctor ordered for our stress relief! "Do not worry" is the powerfully soothing message associated with this flower in the Holy Bible. In Luke 12, Jesus admonishes his disciples not to worry about their lives—what food they will eat and what clothing they will wear. He specifically says to them In verses 27 and 28 (NCV):

> Consider how the lilies grow; they do not work or make clothes for themselves. But I tell you that even Solomon with his riches was not dressed as beautifully as one of these flowers. God clothes the grass in the field, which is alive today and tomorrow is thrown into the fire. So how much more will God clothe you? Don't have so little faith!

It gets even better in verse 32 with "Do not be afraid." I understand that there is a really fine line between being stressed out today and being afraid of the future. However, this biblical, blessed assurance does not do it for all who hear it. This we know, and that is okay. Believing in something more powerful than ourselves is a very personal thing.

Waiting around for manna—or in this case, money—to drop from heaven to avoid foreclosure on the house or repossession of the car is just not the way to go, they would say.

"The age of miracles is past," they would add.

"It's all up to *me*!" they scream.

And the beat goes on: the beat of a palpitating heart, the beat of an Excedrin-induced headache. The noise is deafening!

What was that, again, that Raggedy Ann said? Something about the beauty of lilies making you want to be "ever so quiet, as if you were trying to hear beautiful music coming from far, far away"? Maybe that "beautiful music" is the still, small voice of reason that plays solely for us humans. No other living thing in all of creation possesses this ability to think things through, to fathom and figure out, to consider and conclude, to deduce and decide. The God-given gift of reason is ours alone.

Regarding stress, we have the natural ability to realize when enough is enough, when we have become like a rudderless boat with no direction, constantly going against the currents. Once we slow down long enough (or once we stop to smell the flowers, if you will), then we can put this marvelous ability to work for us. Being reasonable, we can watch our lives go from *distressed* to *de-stressed*!

How wonderful it is to realize that this inherent order so admired in the seasons, the tides, and everything else in nature, is also within us! Keeping our wits about us, being reasonable, can bring to our hurried, harried lives a profound peace. It is all about just being good to ourselves. In her book of daily meditations, *Grace Notes*, Alexandra Stoddard writes of the natural scheme of things and our place within it:

> There is a plan. We are in it. We are in it together. Nature reminds us that there is an order to beauty. There is a reason for everything. Nature does not waste time. Avoid the redundant, the mindless attention to a presumed duty, the dreary false starts. Focus on the true reasons you do what you do. Are there things you can drop because they aren't vital to you and therefore won't survive? Nature reminds us that rootless things die.[8]

Equally sage advice on the same topic comes from American philosopher and naturalist Henry David Thoreau, who conducted an experiment in living at Walden Pond, near his home in Concord, Massachusetts. Thoreau wrote with conviction in his journal, "Why should we live with such hurry and waste of life?… Let us spend one day as deliberately as Nature."[9]

Writing those words in the nineteenth century, Thoreau would be displeased to find that some things never change. Today, we seemingly live with even more "hurry and waste of life" than he witnessed. In fact, the demands upon us have increased over the years while our control over how to meet these demands has lessened. Subsequently, organizing tasks and simplifying lifestyles are really hot topics in the current media. These external sources of help may be good for the stress that ails us; but our own internal resource of reason, a natural gift to each of us, is infinitely the better one, I believe.

Let's think it through. Let's make a list of those things that waste our time, the redundancies, the presumed duties, the false starts that Ms. Stoddard cites. After all, we know our own situations better than anyone else. We know just where we get bogged down, where it starts to get hairy. More importantly, we have what it takes to fix the flaws. We have good *natural* sense.

Most of the books, articles, and workshops devoted to simplifying and organizing our lives are both worthy and effective; but they are mainly for those who can allot the precious *time* to peruse or attend them! It is truly one of those "doomed if I do and doomed if I don't" scenarios, isn't it? How about a crash course? Allow me to share five staples of organization gleaned from my own research on stress relief. These basic principles appeared in some syntactical form or another in almost every source consulted. Perhaps that is because they are so sensible and *reasonable*. Ah, there's that magic word again! Here are the five simple tenets that can help us begin to replace daily chaos and confusion with balance and harmony:

1) Get control of self.
2) Get organized.
3) Delegate.
4) Schedule time. Prioritize.
5) Catch up. Get rid of backlog.

A vital point not yet clarified is the fact that the many sources of human stress are either internal or external. The above suggestions are ways that we can help ourselves to alleviate emotional pressures arising mostly from our *own* scheduling (internal stress), those over which we have control. All the reason and sanity we can muster will not lighten the load shoved on us by an overzealous work supervisor or a well-intentioned mother-in-law (external stress). These call for diplomacy in large doses and just plain coping, I suppose.

However, we can exercise reason in the face of those stressors that begin and end with us. Here are some sensible suggestions aimed at helping us to regain a sense of control in our hectic lives: we can say no when another obligation would put us over the top. We can set more short-term, reachable goals that will delight us rather than too many long-term goals that will only disappoint. By scheduling and prioritizing, we can satisfy our longing to have those things that we value consuming the most of our time. We can surely honor others, including our children, by trusting them to help us. We can stop procrastinating. Laughing at ourselves and smiling at others are good for what ails us and them. Finally, we must remember to pamper ourselves by scheduling downtime—time just for us to soak in a hot bath, curl up with a good book, or walk outside amid the trees and flowers.

Well, it has been a while, but that last suggestion brings us full circle. We are back to where we first began this discussion of stress relief. If you recall, Raggedy Ann had enticed us to stop and smell the flowers and to be still enough to hear the voice of nature. Rearranging our lives so as to become a part of nature's orderly beauty is proof indeed that we have heard the still, small voice of reason. Invoking the lovely Serenity Prayer, attributed to Reinhold Niebuhr, that voice would have us change the things we can, accept the things we cannot change, and be ever thankful for the innate wisdom to know the difference.

I am writing this nature essay in February, in my region's "dead of winter," as the saying goes. If a poll were taken, I daresay that winter would come in fourth among favored seasons by poets and the general populace alike. "Welcome, Springtime" is in reality a seasonal slur—just a nice way of saying, "Winter, begone!" Also, most people are at a complete loss for nice words to describe winter, favoring instead the likes of *cold, barren, dead,* and *void.* I naturally pull for the underdog in most conflicts, so I have not found it difficult to come up with appealing characteristics of winter.

For one thing, the drama of tree silhouettes and the subtle colors and textures of bark are all more apparent in the pale light of winter. This time of year is also the very best time for outer observation and inner reflection. Exchanging urban confines, if need be, for a quiet rural setting on a fine late-winter day can lead to wonderful discoveries. There is a softness about being alone in such a scene, especially if it is snow covered. American poet Robert Frost captured the moment in one of his most famous poems, "Stopping by Woods on a Snowy Evening":

> Whose woods these are I think I know.
> His house is in the village though;
> He will not see me stopping here
> To watch his woods fill up with snow.
>
> My little horse must think it queer
> To stop without a farmhouse near

Between the woods and frozen lake
The darkest evening of the year.

He gives his harness bells a shake
To ask if there is some mistake.
The only other sound's the sweep
Of easy wind and downy flake.

The woods are lovely, dark and deep,
But I have promises to keep,
And miles to go before I sleep,
And miles to go before I sleep.[10]

These beautifully descriptive words make it easy to see why Frost said that a poem begins as a "lump in the throat." I can see this lovely scene just as clearly as if brush had been put to canvas. More than that, I can feel the downy flakes upon my face and eyelashes. I am alone yet surrounded by everything that matters, everything that is good and pure and worth living for. I distinctly hear the harness bells. They become my call to worship in a congregation of one. After a while, swallowing hard, I know that another lesson in Life Appreciation 101 has ended. Giddyap!

Even dolls can be awed by winter's distinctive beauty, it would seem. Here is a description of a scene quite similar, taken from "Making Angels in the Snow," a chapter in *Raggedy Andy Stories*:

"Out across the road from Gran'mas's home, way out in the country, there is a lovely pond," Raggedy Andy explained. "In the summertime pretty flowers grow about the edge, the little green frogs sit upon the pond lilies and beat upon their tiny drums all through the night, and the twinkling stars wink at their reflections in the smooth water. But when Marcella and I went out to Gran'ma's last week, Gran'ma met us with a sleigh, for the ground was covered with starry snow. The pretty pond was covered with ice, too, and upon the ice was a soft blanket of the white, white snow. It was beautiful!" said Raggedy Andy.[11]

Another beautiful sight is nature's most intricate architecture: birds' nests, which are best appreciated against the stark background of late winter. Look but do not disturb, however; for even when deserted, nests of both native and migrant bird species are protected extensively by state and federal laws. Simply put, one needs a *permit* to tamper with the nests or their inhabitants in any season. With this understanding in mind and binoculars in hand, any ornithologist, professional or aspiring, can make great strides in self-education and have great fun with winter nest-hunting. Gone are the leaves of prior seasons that protected the tree nests from the fury of the elements and the gaze of the curious. Now, evacuated and fully exposed are these avian examples of house-building wisdom, stability, and flair.

Driven by the need to be warm, dry, and safe (just like us), the birds build accordingly. Only on rare occasions do nests succumb to high wind or heavy rain, for the little engineers choose their foundations carefully. Many excellent field guides are available in print for anyone desiring facts to go along with the sheer fun of locating birds' nests in winter. To start you looking in earnest and, perhaps, to whet your appetite for more avian knowledge, I proffer these "nesting art" facts: robins generally include a sprig of white, preferably yarn or string; and those worrisome blue jays often weave in a wildflower for a spot of color! Go figure!

Should you happen upon a domicile small and delicate enough to house one of Raggedy Ann's fairy friends, you have a real find and immediate bragging rights. Just two inches in diameter, the home of a hummingbird will reveal itself only to the most devoted of nest seekers. Moreover, in keeping with the little inhabitants' delicacy, the nest will invariably contain the silk of spiders and caterpillars as binder for its minuscule building materials!

Truth be told, winter is despicable because it is, for some, like a wake of three months' duration. Seemingly, all the attributes of death—the pallor, the cold, the silence, the depression—are present in abundance in winter, aren't they? They surround. They encase. Rebellious spirits cry out in alarm and voice their longing for the vibrant colors, the comforting warmth, the busy harbingers of spring. All of this is so very natural, and I do mean *all* of this. Human nature justifiably shuns reminders of life's cessation, even with full understanding by most that dying is a natural part of living. It is the destiny of everything that lives to die at some time.

In Ecclesiastes 3 is that often-quoted passage that begins, "There is a time for everything, and a season for every activity under heaven: a time to be born and a time to die." Nonetheless, it is the nature of us humans to want to control our respective destinies. When death is inevitable after an accident or a terminal illness, the majority still opt for life-sustaining machines to prolong a heartbeat or the breathing process even though life as they knew it is gone. In contrast, a living will, effected prior to the medical crisis, allows one to return in dignity and grace to the natural world from which he or she has come.

Very late last fall, on two separate occasions, I found a big beautiful butterfly (monarch, I believe) lifeless on my driveway. The bodies and wings of both finds were intact. It was as if these symbols of freedom had merely alighted there, as anywhere else, but simply could not rise and go further. They had fulfilled their *raison d'etre*. Their life spans had come full circle.

A Japanese poet would surely have seen these as haiku moments and rendered a verse as startling as the event itself. My own response was less creative but just as satisfying to me. Holding one of the now-stilled butterflies in my palm and stroking its velvety, symmetrically patterned wings, I thought of the sheer joy that its sighting had probably brought to so many in its lifetime. My retrospective mind's eye saw it settle, light as a soap bubble, on the hand of a playing child, filling her first with startled surprise and then with glee. I saw it make a housewife's day by choosing to settle on the pink petunias in the box outside her kitchen window. I thought too of my personal choice some time ago to die as these butterflies had died, taking my last breath in freedom. My own living will never seemed more satisfying than at that moment.

For Johnny Gruelle to have included the topic of human death in one of his children's books in 1929, it was a very courageous endeavor on both a personal and professional level, I believe. It probably was not by chance that one of the eleven stories in his book titled *Marcella* (1929) included an account of a child's dying. The book itself honored his own daughter, Marcella, who had died at age thirteen of an infection following a smallpox vaccination. It is a generally accepted fact that Gruelle's determination to keep alive within his own heart and mind the memory of his beautiful daughter led, directly or indirectly, to the very creation of Raggedy Ann and, subsequently, her many adventures. Moreover, Gruelle's manner of accepting Marcella's death was a wonderful example of the triumph of the human spirit over adversity.

Broaching the subject of dying in *Marcella*, the author, in my thinking, placed himself somewhat against the grain of the advertised slogan of his publisher at the time, the P. F. Volland Company. The slogan read as follows:

> Make your children happy with Volland books. It is the Volland ideal that books for children should contain nothing to cause fright, suggest fear, glorify mischief, extenuate malice, or condone

cruelty. That is why they are called 'books good for children.'

Arguably, also, Gruelle risked inciting the ire of protective parents who were seeking, understandably, to shield their innocent children from any reference to death or dying. That such did not happen after the publication of *Marcella* is indeed a credit to the author's superb handling of the subject of death in the chapter entitled "Through the Door."

For comfort's sake (his own and that of his young audience), I like to think that Gruelle purposefully cast in this chapter his four most recognizable story dolls. "Raggedy Ann and Raggedy Andy and Beloved Belindy and Uncle Clem were sitting out in the playhouse,"[12] reads the very first sentence of "Through the Door." Even more comfort comes from Gruelle's setting the scene with lovely, natural description:

> The sun went down and the evening shadows turned everything to a lovely purple, and the little fire-flies with their twinkling lanterns came up out of the grass and sailed high into the air.[13]

Raggedy Ann herself supplies some plot foreshadowing by exclaiming, "Who knows, Beloved Belindy… Perhaps we may see the fairies!"[14]

Gruelle adds just a bit of mystery for good measure: "Something like a twig snapping was heard near the orchard fence… They [the four dolls] drew back into the playhouse and waited as the sounds came closer."[15] For his plot's main thrust, the writer wisely chooses a situation dear to the heart of any child, a puppy dog's love for its little master. Once established, this plotline develops almost poetically, complete with that Frostian "lump in the throat." The story's denouement has a very tired puppy dog simply "going to sleep," as announced by a whispering Belindy; it is an ever-so-natural occurrence that a child may grasp effortlessly. Simultaneously, the following natural phenomenon happens:

> At first it sounded to the four dolls as if a gentle breeze blew softly across silken strings, breathing a soft, half-heard melody. Then as it grew louder, but still soft and fairylike, the dolls all held their cotton-stuffed breaths and waited. A light, as if hundreds of fireflies were banded together, came across the grass of the orchard and the faint sound the dolls had heard was the soft singing of tiny fairies.[16]

Neither the writer nor the puppy dog is yet finished, however. What ensues in the concluding page and a half of "Through the Door" is a reunion guaranteed to make the eyes of real-for-sure people, just like Raggedy Ann's shoe-button eyes, "shiny with happiness." Perhaps you should read it and weep…for joy.

With forewarning, I have now given much space to winter and even waxed poetic about it; and I am fully content in this discourse on nature to slight the other three seasons. Nevertheless, they do not go unheralded. The poets take good care of springtime, personifying it as youth itself with all its accompanying energy, spontaneity, and charm. Every schoolchild (and teacher) knows that summer is spelled v-a-c-a-t-i-o-n. Just follow the bouncing beach ball! Young and old alike welcome fall's change of pace in a melancholy sort of way. Football players and marching bands and yards of leaves will keep them all busy until winter once more says, "Shhhh…"

Varied as the four seasons are for enjoyable human activity, they share one thing in common that is anything but pleasurable. Each has its own natural force or forces with which we humans must contend, ready or not. As Emily Dickinson so aptly put it, "Nature, like us, is sometimes caught without her diadem." Indeed, there is nothing regal about a flood, an earthquake, a tornado, an ice storm, or a hurricane. Lives are lost in the terrible wake of these forces, along with houses and land and hope.

Facing all the death, destruction, and despair heaped upon us by nature periodically, we are always shocked, surprised, and puzzled. I wonder, *Why is this?* Should we humans not know by now that we cannot control nature? Does she not get from us the respect that she deserves? Historian Thomas DiBacco believes not.

> Bad weather in modern America has a far more dramatic and costly impact than it did earlier in history when there were fewer buildings and fewer densely

populated areas. Why? Because early Americans showed a healthier respect for nature and planned for it. Contemporary society is apt to pay less heed to weather, thinking instead that man and technology are paramount.[17]

Each of these devastating phenomena has occurred many, many times before and can be fully expected to recur simply because they are natural forces. In truth, meteorological technology contributes much to the preparedness process in a physical sense, but nothing can soften the emotional blow of losing hearth and home. The best we humans can do in the face of natural disasters is just what we have watched each other do time and time again: cope and carry on.

"Why did God let this happen?" is a question often heard amid the chaos surrounding one of the natural disasters cited above. The reasoning is that so much force and fury could come only from the Almighty. Sorry to disappoint, but the God I know and love would no more blow up a strong wind and wipe out a sleeping family than he would put a repeating rifle in the hand of an irrational employee to wipe out innocents in the workplace. There is order and balance and harmony in nature, remember? Things go wrong, terribly wrong, when the order and balance and harmony are somehow disturbed and disrupted, whether by too much warm and cold air mixing in the atmosphere or by something snapping in a human's brain.

God has an abiding place, but it is not within nature's wrath. The Bible tells me so in 1 Kings 19:11,12 (NCV):

> Then a very strong wind blew until it caused the mountains to fall apart and shattered the rocks. But the Lord was not in the wind. After the wind there was an earthquake, but the Lord was not in the earthquake. After the earthquake came a fire, but the Lord was not in the fire. And after the fire came a quiet, gentle sound.

So if we take him at his Word, God is *not* in the wind and earthquake but in the still, small voice that abides within us all. It is the voice of reason that leads us to better understand the natural world of which we are a part.

Harsh as it may seem at this moment, let's attempt to be fair in this assessment of nature's malevolence. What of the things that we humans do to Mother Earth? Are they all good and right and needed? Some are, like irrigation or diverting water for drinking; but more are not, like wasting trees as if they could magically replenish themselves, or daily poisoning the air and water. In these and in a myriad of other ways, we change the environment to suit us; and for the most part, nature goes along with this human manipulation. Every now and then, however, nature rises up in ways that serve almost as a pithy reminder of just *who* is in charge here. Needless to say, she gets our attention.

There is a unique compilation titled *The Nature of Nature: New Essays from America's Finest Writers on Nature*.

One of the contributors, David E. Fisher, makes this bold assertion:

> Though we are part of and one with nature, we are not merely one more species among billions of others; we have developed a complex consciousness capable of understanding the universe, and with even the beginnings of this understanding comes the ability to manipulate… Unfortunately…hubris…leads us to think that we can not only manipulate but actually conquer the universe…
>
> We must strive to understand the world we live in; we must demystify the nature of nature. I think that when we do we will find that she is neither evil nor beneficent but simply uncaring; that we as a species are immaterial to her; that she could not care less if we thrive or shrivel, if we exist or join the dinosaurs in oblivion…
>
> It's time to face up to the fact that even our own earth doesn't care whether we live or die. For if we douse the world in radioactivity or warm it beyond the temperatures of all past climates in greenhouse gases, nature will yet endure. As conditions change, nature will change with them and go on as serenely as before. If some species disappear, well, that's all in

the scheme of things... It matters not one whit to nature.

Ay, there's the rub. For if we change nature sufficiently, we may find that we are no longer welcome on this planet. And so, we had better tread softly, until we understand better how nature works and how we fit into the nature of things.[18]

Well, I did warn you that it was bold. Fisher's "treading softly" can be interpreted as being more environmentally aware, more ecologically conscious. Taking care of our earth is the right thing to do, whether we do so out of fear of extinction or gratitude for creation, or a blend of both. It does no good merely to fret about the loss of topsoil, ozone depletion, strip-mined hills, endangered species, and acidified lakes.

Action and action alone—lifestyle change—makes a person part of the solution. Until then, he or she remains a part of the critical issue of the human species: the overpopulation of our planet earth. Something as simple as opting to use real plates and cups instead of throwaways, buying recycled paper whenever possible, or avoiding aerosol containers on a regular basis, will be a wonderful start toward personally helping our wounded natural world.

At this point, you will have to agree that a discussion of nature can become as big as all outdoors, huh? In trying to come by a way to conclude this particular essay, to wind up "Sunny Bunny," so to speak, I happened to recall something that Raggedy Ann once said about the varied sounds, the music, of nature. She said, "It's just like a great, great big music box which old Mister Sun winds up every evening before he goes to bed, so that it will start bright and early in the morning playing and sending out happy sounds for everyone's pleasure."[19] (*Raggedy Ann's Wishing Pebble*, 1925).

Well, I'm no Mister Sun {not bright enough}, but I have tried within these pages to send out some natural sounds that will reverberate in your mind and heart for a long time to come. Want to hum along? Raggedy Ann surely does!

The last, best *Word* on Nature is from Psalm 8:3–9 (NCV):

> I look at your heavens, which you made with your fingers. I see the moon and stars, which you created. But why are people even important to you? Why do you take care of human beings? You made them a little lower than the angels and crowned them with glory and honor. You put them in charge of everything you made. You put all things under their control: all the sheep, the cattle, and the wild animals, the birds in the sky, the fish in the sea, and everything that lives under water. Lord, our Lord, your name is the most wonderful name in all the earth!

Endnotes

Marcella

1. Kahlil Gibran, *The Broken Wings* (New York: Meraat-ul-Gharb, 1912).
2. Pope John Paul I, "Angelus," (prayer, The Vatican, September 10, 1978), ©Libreria Editrice Vaticana.
3. Robert F. Capon, *Bed and Board: Plain Talk about Marriage* (New York: Simon and Schuster, Inc., 1965).
4. Johnny Gruelle, *Raggedy Ann Stories* (Chicago: The P.F. Volland Company, 1918), 72–74.
5. Gruelle, *Raggedy Ann Stories,* 81.
6. Gruelle, *Raggedy Ann Stories*, 66.
7. Johnny Gruelle, *Raggedy Ann in the Deep Deep Woods* (Joliet: Volland, 1930), 85.
8. John Vaughan, "A Mother and a Baby: Life's Wondrous Miracle," *The Charlotte Observer*, May 10, 1998, A, 1,14.
9. Vaughan, *A Mother and a Baby: Life's Wondrous Miracle*. A,1.
10. Benjamin Spock, M.D., *Baby and Child Care* (New York: Duell, Sloan and Pearce, 1946).
11. Washington Irving (1783–1859).
12. Johnny Gruelle, *Friendly Fairies* (Chicago: Volland, 1919), 51.
13. Gruelle, *Friendly Fairies*, 52.
14. George Cooper (1840–1927).
15. "Grandparents Raising Grandchildren: The School Connection," https://assets.aarp.org./articles /families/school_ connection.
16. *All My Children*. ABC. WSOC, Charlotte. December 24, 1997. Television.
17. "Employment Characteristics of Families Summary," www.bls.gov/news.release/famee.nr0.htm.
18. Judith Viorst, *Necessary Losses: The Loves, Illusions, Dependencies and Impossible Expectations That All of Us Have to Give Up in Order to Grow* (New York: Simon & Schuster, 1986), 21.
19. Johnny Gruelle, *Raggedy Ann and the Happy Meadow* (Indianapolis: The Bobbs-Merrill Company, 1961), 91.

Rags

1. Johnny Gruelle, *Raggedy Ann Stories* (Chicago: Volland, 1918), 21.
2. Johnny Gruelle, *Raggedy Ann's Wishing Pebble* (Joliet: Volland, 1925), 21.
3. Gruelle, *Raggedy Ann Stories*, 56.
4. Gruelle, *Raggedy Ann Stories*, 56.
5. Gruelle, *Raggedy Ann Stories*, 60.
6. Johnny Gruelle, *Orphant Annie Story Book* (Indianapolis: Bobbs-Merrill, 1921), 3.
7. Johnny Gruelle, *Raggedy Ann and the Golden Ring* (Indianapolis: Bobbs-Merrill, 1961), 27.
8. Gruelle, *Orphant Annie Story Book*, 20.
9. Johnny Gruelle, *Raggedy Ann and Andy and the Camel with the Wrinkled Knees* (Joliet: Volland, 1924), 88.
10. Florence May Alt, "My Life Is but a Weaving," *The Troy Weekly Times*, May 6, 1892.
11. Johnny Gruelle, *Raggedy Ann's Lucky Pennies* (Joliet: Volland, 1932), 16.

Pirate Chieftain

1. Johnny Gruelle, *The Paper Dragon: A Raggedy Ann Adventure* (Joliet: Volland, 1926), ch.5.
2. Johnny Gruelle, *Raggedy Andy Stories* (Chicago: Volland, 1920), 76.
3. Gruelle, *The Paper Dragon*, ch. 8.
4. Johnny Gruelle, *Raggedy Ann and the Hobby Horse* (Indianapolis: Bobbs-Merrill, 1961), 42.
5. Johnny Gruelle, *Raggedy Ann and the Nice Fat Policeman* (New York: The Johnny Gruelle Company, 1942), 36.
6. Johnny Gruelle, *Raggedy Ann Stories* (Chicago: Volland, 1918), 40.
7. Carl Sandburg, "Primer Lesson," in *Smoke and Steel and Slabs of the Sunburnt West*, (New York: Harcourt Brace and Company, 1921).
8. Susan Heitler, PhD, *From Conflict to Resolution* (New York: W.W. Norton & Co., Inc., 1990).
9. Gruelle, *The Paper Dragon*, ch.10.
10. Johnny Gruelle, *Raggedy Ann and Andy's Sunny Stories*, a compilation (New York: Bobbs-Merrill, 1974), 24.
11. Gruelle, *Raggedy Ann and Andy's Sunny Stories*.
12. Johnny Gruelle, *Raggedy Ann's Wishing Pebble* (Joliet: Volland, 1925), 4.
13. Gruelle, *The Paper Dragon*, ch.1.
14. Ann Landers (Esther Pauline "Eppie" Lederer, 1918–2002).
15. Landers.
16. Gruelle, *The Paper Dragon*, ch.6.

ENDNOTES

Thomas

1. Johnny Gruelle, *Raggedy Ann Stories* (Chicago: Volland, 1918), 61.
2. Johnny Gruelle, *Raggedy Ann and Andy and the Camel with the Wrinkled Knees* (Joliet: Volland, 1924), 18.
3. Johnny Gruelle, *Raggedy Andy Stories* (Chicago: Volland, 1920), 16.
4. Nicholas Sparks, *The Notebook* (Boston: Hachette Book Group, 1996), 2.
5. H. L. Mencken (1880–1956).
6. M. Scott Peck, *The Road Less Traveled: A New Psychology of Love, Traditional Values, and Spiritual Growth* (New York: Simon & Schuster, Inc., 1978), 91.
7. Peck, *The Road Less Traveled: A New Psychology of Love, Traditional Values, and Spiritual Growth*, 104.
8. Helen Steiner Rice, "The Meaning of True Love," in *Showers of Blessings* (Tarrytown: The Fleming H. Revell Company, 1980), 51.
9. Johnny Gruelle, *The Paper Dragon: A Raggedy Ann Adventure* (Joliet: Volland, 1926), ch.11.
10. Gruelle, *Raggedy Andy Stories*, 80.
11. Gruelle, *Raggedy Ann Stories*, 86.

Percy the Policeman

1. Patricia Hall, *Johnny Gruelle: Creator of Raggedy Ann and Andy* (Gretna: Pelican Publishing Co., Inc.,1993), 197.
2. Johnny Gruelle, *Raggedy Ann's Wishing Pebble* (Joliet: Volland, 1925), 95.
3. Johnny Gruelle, *Raggedy Ann and the Golden Ring*, (New York: Bobbs-Merrill, 1961), 24.

Eddie Elephant

1. Johnny Gruelle, *The Paper Dragon: A Raggedy Ann Adventure* (Joliet: Volland, 1926), ch.10.
2. Johnny Gruelle, *Raggedy Andy Stories* (Chicago: Volland, 1920), 84.
3. Johnny Gruelle, *Raggedy Ann and the Golden Ring*, (New York: Bobbs-Merrill, 1961), 51.
4. Madeline Bridges (1844–1920), "Life's Mirror," in *Love Songs and Other Poems*, 1870.
5. Barbara Kingsolver, *Animal Dreams* (New York: HarperCollins Publishing, 1990).

6. Gruelle, *Raggedy Andy Stories*, 16.
7. C. S. Lewis, *A Grief Observed* (New York: Seabury Press, 1961).
8. Charles Frazier, *Cold Mountain* (New York: Grove Atlantic, 1997).
9. Alzheimer's Association, "2020 Alzheimer's Disease Facts and Figures."
10. Gruelle, *The Paper Dragon*, ch. 11.
11. James M. Barrie, author (1860–1937).

The Little Brown Bear

1. Johnny Gruelle, *The Paper Dragon: A Raggedy Ann Adventure* (Joliet: Volland, 1926), ch.5.
2. Johnny Gruelle, *Raggedy Ann's Wishing Pebble* (Joliet: Volland, 1925), 31.
3. "Americans Still Overweight but More Stop Smoking: Poll," Reuters Lifeline, March 2018, https://www.reuters.com/article/us-survey-idUSN0562628920080305.
4. Maggie Fox, "American Obesity Rates Are on the Rise, Gallop Poll Finds," May 27, 2015, https://www.nbcnews.com/better/diet-fitness/we-re-getting-even-fatter-survey-finds-n365276.
5. "Obese Patients Have Higher Health Care Costs Than Nonobese," *Science Daily*, https://www.sciencedaily.com/release/200410/041030.
6. Johnny Gruelle, *Raggedy Andy Stories* (Chicago: Volland, 1920), 56.
7. "How Much Sugar Do You Eat?" https://www.dhhs.nh.gov/dphs/nhp/documents/sugar.pdf.
8. Jennifer Kelly Geddes, "Everything You Need to Know about Chromium," *Everyday Health*, May 1, 2019, https://www.everydayhealth.com/diet-nutrition/all-about-chromium.

Sunny Bunny

1. Johnny Gruelle, *Raggedy Ann and the Happy Meadow* (Indianapolis: Bobbs-Merrill, 1961), 45.
2. Johnny Gruelle, *Marcella: A Raggedy Ann Story* (Joliet: Volland, 1929), 36.
3. Johnny Gruelle, *Raggedy Ann in the Deep Deep Woods* (Joliet: Volland, 1930), 7.
4. Gruelle, *Raggedy Ann in the Deep Deep Woods*, 70.
5. Gruelle, *Happy Meadow*, 74.
6. William Wordsworth (1770–1850), "The Tables Turned," in *Lyrical Ballads*, 1798.
7. Gruelle, *Happy Meadow*, 43–5.
8. Alexandra Stoddard, *Grace Notes* (New York: Harper Collins, 1993), 124.
9. Henry David Thoreau (1817–1862), *Walden: Life in the Woods*, 1854.

ENDNOTES

10. Robert Frost (1874–1963), "Stopping by Woods on a Snowy Evening," *The Poetry of Robert Frost* (New York: Henry Holt Co., 1923).
11. Johnny Gruelle, *Raggedy Andy Stories* (Chicago: Volland, 1920), 84.
12. Gruelle, *Marcella*, 65.
13. Gruelle, *Marcella*, 65.
14. Gruelle, *Marcella*, 65.
15. Gruelle, *Marcella*, 66.
16. Gruelle, *Marcella*, 68–9.
17. Thomas DiBacco, "Learning Again It's Not Nice to Ignore Mother Nature," *The Baltimore Sun*, January 14, 1996, https://www.baltimoresun.com/news/bs-xpm-1996-01-14-19960114-story-html.
18. David E. Fisher, "The Nature of Nature," in *The Nature of Nature: New Essays from America's Finest Writers on Nature*, edited by William H. Shore, (San Diego: Harcourt Brace, 1995), 140–1.
19. Johnny Gruelle, *Raggedy Ann's Wishing Pebble*, (Joliet: Volland, 1925), 22.

About the Author

Cozette Stacy Nowak is a native of North Carolina, where she counseled and taught creative writing and literature to high school students for twenty plus years. She recalls the profession fondly as more of a joy than a job. A self-described intellectual "vagabond," she has enjoyed her wanderings across the vast landscape of human possibility, seeking always to expand the limits of her abilities. As Mrs. South Carolina Senior 2002, Cozette afterward received a proclamation at the State House in Columbia for her year of service as goodwill ambassador. She resides in South Carolina with her husband, Johnny, and their perennial houseguest, Raggedy Ann.

CPSIA information can be obtained
at www.ICGtesting.com
Printed in the USA
LVHW070724060222
710384LV00030B/735